THE APPLEY BRIDGE METEORITE

RUSSELL PARRY

Advanced Food Safety
LIMITED
INTERNATIONAL FOOD SAFETY CONSULTANTS AND TRAINERS

This book is dedicated to two people.
My father, Roy Parry, who stood out with me star gazing on cold winter nights and encouraged my love of astronomy and science and to the late Sir Patrick Moore who inspired and introduced me and many of my generation to the wonders of the universe.

First published 2014 by Advanced Food Safety Limited

Jubilee House, 5 Broad O'th Lane, Shevington, Wigan, Lancashire WN6 8EA
Tel: 01257 254999 Fax: 01257 254888
Email: info@food-safety.co.uk • Web: www.food-safety.co.uk

ISBN 978-0-9549531-2-6

1st edition October 2014

1 3 5 7 9 8 6 4 2

A CIP catalogue record for this book is available from the British Library.

ACKNOWLEDGEMENTS

I would like to thank the following people and organisations for their help and support in writing this book

Deborah-Jayne Cassey - The Natural History Museum London
Dr Caroline Smith - Natural History Museum London
Kate Tyte - Natural History Museum London
Kate Sherburn - The Manchester Museum
Dr David Gelsthorpe - The Manchester Museum
Barry Henshall - Manchester Astronomical Society
Tracy Warmington - Harvard Mineralogical & Geological Museum USA
Pamela Salyer - Smithsonian Institution Washington, D.C. USA
Dr. Rhiannon Mayne - Curator of the Monnig Meteorite Collection, Texas Christian University USA
Paul P. Sipiera - The Field Museum Chicago USA
Katharine Hassall - Manchester Literary and Philosophical Society
Sergeant Phil Turner courtesy of the Lancashire Constabulary.
Rita Musa - Museum of Wigan Life
Brian and Barbara McDonald for the photos of shop in Appley Bridge
Valerie and David Edwards
Knutsford Library
Roy and Betty Parry
Mark Chivers - Meridian Publications Ltd

Cover image and page 12 by Pavely Arts
Designed by Meridian Publications Ltd
Printed in the UK by Stephens and George

CONTENTS

FOREWORD

I have always loved the story of the Appley Bridge meteorite. Often the most obscure specimens in the museum have some of the most interesting tales.

The beautiful cast of the meteorite and fragment of rock we have on display give a tangible link to the events of October the 13th 1914.

The excitement and fear people must have experienced as it shot across the sky! Then the realisation that the First World War hadn't reached Cheshire after all, but an extra-terrestrial lump of rock was the culprit. Subsequently, research and public interest has ensured its place in history.

Russell Parry has undertaken dedicated research to bring all the elements of this story together. His enthusiasm and interest shine through.

Dr. David Gelsthorpe
Curator of Earth Science Collections
The Manchester Museum

INTRODUCTION

A fascinating tale to tell

I moved from the market town of Shrewsbury in Shropshire to the village of Appley Bridge in Lancashire in 1991 and being new to the area I soon read up on the local history and places of interest around and about.

I READ about the Appley Bridge meteorite in the local history section of Wigan library and having a keen interest in astronomy since I was a boy it captured my imagination. It was one of the largest meteorite falls in Great Britain and it just happened to land outside the village where I now lived.

In 1997, a local village publication, *The Appley Bridge Year Book*, included an article on the meteorite and this prompted me to find out more information on this fascinating event. Over the years I researched the story, unearthing more facts and figures as time went on.

It came to a stage in 2013 that I decided that I must start to produce a book on my findings so that anyone interested can share in this fascinating story. During my research I also found out that the meteorite, shortly after it was found, went on display in my next door neighbour's house, which at the time was the village shop.

Maybe today the same incident would only just have a brief mention in the news, but take a step back in time to October 1914, the meteorite fall, the explosions as it entered the atmosphere, and the confusion with an enemy zeppelin airship or aircraft dropping bombs, all caused great concern. Remember, the Great War, World War 1, had only just started with Great Britain declaring war on Germany in August 1914.

This was a time when flight was in its infancy, with the first powered flight only just under 11 years earlier by the Wright brothers, motor cars had only been on the roads in Great Britain since the mid 1890s and the famous model T Ford was only introduced in 1908. The world was a much quieter, slower place and it was in this environment that the meteorite appeared, exploded and came to earth in a field near Appley Bridge on Tuesday 13th October 1914 at approximately 8.45 pm and discovered the following day.

This is the story of the meteorite fall through archive documents and newspaper reports of the time.

CHAPTER 1

Meteoroids, meteors and meteorites – what are they?

There is often confusion over what meteoroids, meteors and meteorites are. In fact, they are all linked.

LET'S START with meteoroids. A meteoroid is a solid object that is typically 10µm (0.01mm) to 1 metre in size, moving in interplanetary space. Meteoroids are made up of the same materials we find in planets, asteroids and comets and travel through the vacuum of space at an incredible speed, estimated to be between 11 to 72 kilometers per second (7 to 45 miles per second, that's is an incredible 25,000 mph to over 160,000 mph). When these high speed meteoroids enter the Earth' s atmosphere the friction and energy released generates the light we can see when the meteoroid becomes a meteor or what we commonly call a shooting star.

If you stand out and observe the night sky, ideally in an area with as little light pollution as possible late at night or in the early hours of the morning, you will probably see a shooting star. This is a meteor, and 'sporadic' meteors can be observed at anytime. It is usually observed as a short flash of light across the sky, and it is gone in seconds.

At certain times of the year we have what we call meteor showers, these can be predicted with accuracy and are fascinating to observe. Examples of meteor showers are the Quadrantids meteor shower which peaks 2nd to 3rd January, the Perseids meteor shower on 12th August (which some say was connected to the Appley Bridge meteorite), the Leonids meteor shower between the 16th to 17th November and the Geminids meteor shower, which can be one of the most spectacular, and can be observed on the 13th to 14th December. Meteor showers are named after the constellation in the night sky from where the meteors appear to come from. A number of meteor showers are also linked to comets. As the earth travels through the orbit of some comet tails, the particles and debris from the tail enter the atmosphere of the Earth and again burn up causing a display of meteors.

When the particles enter the Earth's atmosphere they simply burn up due to the particles entering the more dense atmosphere and the pressure of entering the atmosphere generates heat and causes light to be emitted, and we can see this on earth as a shooting star. Various colours of light can also be produced depending on the chemical composition of the meteor. They burn up high in the atmosphere in the region called the Mesosphere which is between approximately 50 km and 80 km (30 miles and 50 miles) above the surface of the Earth.

Meteorites are meteors which survive entry through the atmosphere and actually hit the surface of the Earth. They survive entry because they are larger in mass and do not completely burn up. The Appley Bridge meteorite is unusual in the fact that this is classified as a 'fall'. A 'fall' means the meteorite was actually observed falling and then found, as we will be describing in this book. This is what makes the Appley Bridge meteorite unique, as a 'fall' is quite an unusual event.

Although much larger, the meteorite which landed in Chelyabinsk in Russia on 15th February 2013 was also a 'fall', with its dramatic fall to earth and explosions observed on entry into the atmosphere as it was caught on many in-car cameras and CCTV cameras and of course became headline news around the world.

Meteorite strikes can also be a danger to life, the Chelyabinsk meteorite injured an estimated 1500 people and you can see how devastating meteorite landings can be by just looking at images of the famous Barringer Crater in Arizona USA which was caused by a meteorite. The demise of the dinosaurs which once roamed the Earth is also attributed to a major impact by a meteorite.

KNOW YOUR METEORITE

Meteorites are of three main types:

Stone. These are the most common.

Stony iron. These are the rarest type of meteorite which are made up of iron, nickel and silicates. These are divided into two groups. Pallasites, which are mixtures of asteroidal core and mantle material, and according to the latest thinking, may actually represent core-mantle mixtures formed by impacts. The other group are Mesosiderites, it is not completely clear on how these are formed. However, one theory is that they formed by low-velocity impacts of core fragments with the surface of an asteroid.

Iron. As the name suggests the composition is made up of iron together with nickel and they originate from the cores of asteroids.

The most common meteorites we find on earth tend to be of the stony type. Meteorites of the stony category are categorised further into another two types, Achondrites and Chondrites.

Chondrites are the most unchanged meteorites since they were formed at the birth of the solar system which was some 4,560 million years ago. This is why the study of meteorites is so important, as they can provide valuable information regarding the formation of the solar system.

Chondrites are classified into groups and clans based on:

1. Chemical composition.
2. Oxygen isotopic compositions (this maybe the most important because the abundance of the three isotopes of oxygen in a meteorite will provide the best evidence for its classification).
3. Oxidation states (which reveals differences in the proportions of olivine and pyroxene – important mineral constituents of chondrules).
4. Certain physical characteristics (e.g., size of chondrules, degree of metamorphism, etc.).

Chondrules are some of the most primitive objects in the solar system, they are believed to have originated as small molten dust particles, possibly within solar nebula which have cooled and solidified and appear as inclusions in meteorites. Chondrules range in size from a few microns to over 1cm.

The chemical composition and the characteristics of the meteorites gives rise to the classification of the Carbonaceous , Ordinary, Enstatite, Rumurutiites and the Kakangari chondrites.

The Appley Bridge meteorite is classed as an Ordinary Chondrite and these as well as Carbonaceous and Enstatite chondrites are sub-divided further, again on the basis of the chemical composition as stated above.

Ordinary Chondrites are divided into three Groups and each is given a letter designation and a number. The letters designating the groups refer to the bulk iron content as follows:

H chondrites have high total iron contents.
L chondrites have low total iron contents.
LL chondrites have low metallic iron relative to total iron, as well as low total iron contents.

For ordinary chondrites, the number following the chemical class letter designation represents the petrologic type or degree of thermal processing, with lower numbers indicating less alteration.

H		**L**		**LL**	
Abundant	H3-H3.9	Abundant	L3-L3.9	Abundant	LL3-LL3.9
Distinct	H4	Distinct	L4	Distinct	LL4
Less distinct	H5	Less distinct	L5	Less distinct	LL5
Indistinct	H6	Indistinct	L6	Indistinct	LL6
Recrystalized	H7	Recrystalized	L7	Recrystalized	LL7

The Appley Bridge meteorite has a classification of **LL6**. This being a stony, ordinary chondrite, low iron, low metal with indistinct chondrules.

Achondrites are meteorites which do not contain chondrules. These can originate from asteroids, from the planet Mars or from the Moon. These are igneous or melted rocks and have therefore been subjected to heat. There are also various classifications of Achondrite meteorites.

So a meteoroid becomes a meteor when it enters the Earth's atmosphere and a meteor becomes a meteorite if it lands on Earth. Meteorites usually take the name of where they land or are found, hence the Appley Bridge meteorite, found just outside the Lancashire village itself.

LEFT
Meteorites usually take the name of where they land or are found.

© Russell Parry

CHAPTER 2

The story of the Appley Bridge meteorite

Our story starts not on 13th October 1914 when the Appley Bridge meteorite fell to Earth, but 4,560 million years ago. That's 4.6 billion years if you want to round it up!

SO 4.6 BILLION years ago, forming out of nebula gas clouds and debris, was our own solar system. Following the formation of our sun, the gas and dust particles which were left in orbit of the sun collided and formed together to produce what we call planetesimals, these went on to create the planets of our solar system.

Some meteorites are formed as a result of collisions between asteroids which were produced at the same time, from the remains of the birth of our solar system. As some meteorites have not been subject to high temperature and their structures left changed, you can understand why meteorites are so important in studying the formation of the solar system.

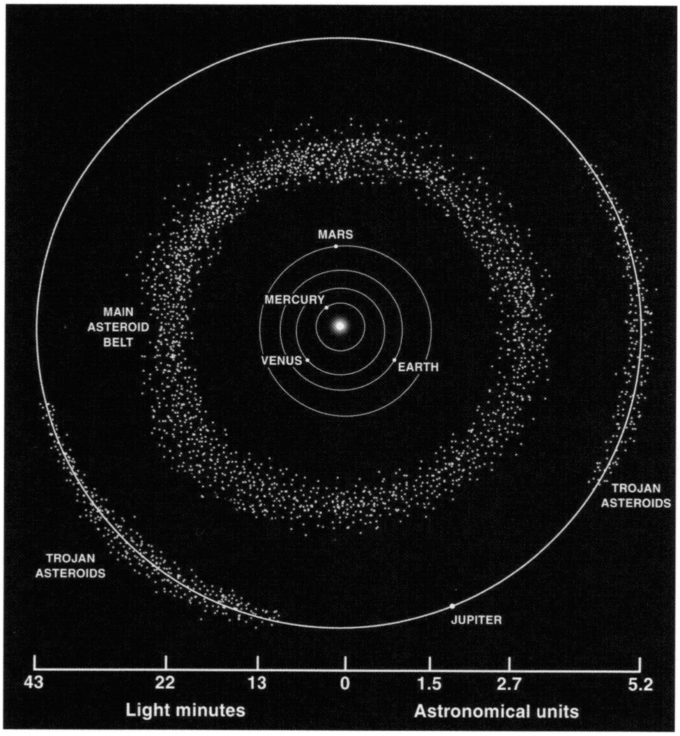

RIGHT The location of the main asteroid belt between the orbits of Mars and Jupiter.

© NASA Lunar and Planetary Institute

Therefore, the Appley Bridge meteorite had been travelling around in space all this time. Our meteorite could have been part of a larger asteroid which was in orbit around the sun in what we call the asteroid belt. The asteroid belt is situated between the orbits of Mars and Jupiter, roughly 186 million to 370 million miles (300 million to 600 million kilometers) from the Sun.

Following collisions between asteroids, meteors and meteorites would have been formed and would have been flung out and sent on a different orbit around the sun. This resulted in the Appley Bridge meteorite ultimately being on a collision course with the Earth.

DRAMATIC APPEARANCE

So after 4.6 billion years travelling through space the Appley Bridge meteorite made its dramatic appearance. First appearing directly over Stoke on Trent and travelling the 49 miles over Cheshire and into Lancashire, landing in a field on the outskirts of Appley Bridge. The newspaper reports of the time provide us with vivid accounts of the actual sightings which we have documented in the next chapter.

The meteorite fall was actually found by two gentlemen described in the newspapers of the time as 'sportsmen', one being an employee of Halliwell Farm where the meteorite was found, the farm at that time extended to some 140 acres.

As the two gentlemen were walking the fields on the outskirts of Appley Bridge on the morning after the meteorite fall, they may have been discussing the events of the previous evening, the fireball and tail in the sky and the claps of thunder like explosions. Was it an enemy Zeppelin after all? Or was it the reported aeroplane dropping bombs on the nearby army camp at Winstanley?

LEFT
Halliwell Farm possibly taken in the early 1900s.

Photo courtesy of Valerie and David Edwards

2

RIGHT: Halliwell Farm as it is today.

It is likely they were discussing the events of the previous evening as it was seen by hundreds of people in the local Wigan area and lit up the night sky as it headed in a Northerly direction. One account even said that Dr J H Wilson, a resident of Standish and the medical officer for the district, had spoken to numerous residents in Appley Bridge and many of them used the expression that although it was night they could "see to pick up a pin by the light given out." Local residents also reported the "buzzing of the engines of the Zeppelin".

RIGHT: Digging out the meteorite after the find.

© Russell Parry

Only a reported 3 minutes walk away from the farm buildings, the two gentlemen noticed what they thought was a hare or rabbit, another report suggested it was an upturned mound of earth which caught their eye. On approaching it they soon discovered this was no rabbit or hare, they had discovered the landing place of the meteorite embedded in the earth in a hole approximately 2 feet across and 18 inches deep and in it, the dark red mass of the meteorite broken into two pieces. On getting a spade from the nearby farm, Halliwell Farm, they set about digging it out. Some reports saying it was dug out by the farmer himself Mr Eric Lyon. The meteorite was then taken back to the farmhouse.

LEFT
1920 Rural District Map showing the following districts around the area of the meteorite fall:

Pink = Wrightington
Green = Dalton
Yellow = Parbold
Blue = Shevington
White = Upholland

Provided courtesy of Wigan Archives & Local Studies WLCT

With the meteorite landing within 3 minutes walk of Halliwell Farm (see maps) the fall was nearer to the village of Appley Bridge than any other village of a reasonable size, but there is a dispute over claims to the meteorite from the Dalton and Upholland Districts. The name is officially the Appley Bridge meteorite of course, but looking at this map, Halliwell Farm is clearly in the district of Upholland.

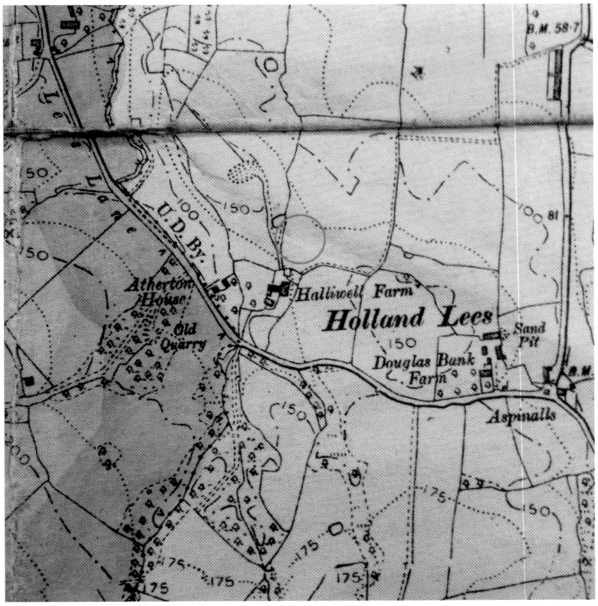

LEFT
Close up of the 1920 Rural District Map showing the location of Halliwell Farm. The red circle indicates the 3 minute walk from the farmhouse as paced out during my visit to the farmhouse. It was in this area that the meteorite fell.

Provided courtesy of Wigan Archives & Local Studies WLCT

2

Dr Wilson, the medical officer for the district, visited Mr Lyon at the farmhouse and inspected the object. He provided a description to a local newspaper as follows: "The mass is just like a large stone, irregular in shape, and externally of a reddish colour similar to the appearance of rusty iron, or of iron drawn from a fire. It is also very friable." He went on to say: "pieces can be broken from it by the fingers alone. Internally the prevailing colour is that of French grey, the material is of varying hardness, and some parts having the resemblance of lead. It is about 30 inches in circumference and weighs about 30lbs."

TOP RIGHT This is the first motor car owned by the Lancashire Constabulary, pictured with driver Special Constable James Rossall. The photograph was taken in 1914. Could this be the police car that was sent to collect the Appley Bridge meteorite from Halliwell Farm?

Courtesy of the Lancashire Constabulary

THE POLICE TAKE CHARGE

The police were informed of the find and Superintendent Kelly of the Wigan County Police visited Halliwell Farm by motor car and promptly confiscated the meteorite on behalf of the Mr H H Lane (whose actual name was Philip Lane, but known as Harry), the Chief Constable of Lancashire County. The meteorite was then taken to the County Policy Headquarters in Preston for investigation and examination.

Superintendent Kelly later gave an interview to the local newspapers and stated that the find entirely dispels the idea of an airship passing over the district. The fallen body he said weighed some 30lbs and is heavier than it looks. On the outside it is dark brown in colour like rust iron and is covered with a sort of burnt powder. Inside the colour is light grey with spots of gold and bright coloured metals. There is no doubt, the Superintendent added, that it is a genuine meteorite.

RIGHT Sir Philip Lane (known as Harry Lane), Chief Constable of Lancashire, who ordered the confiscation of the meteorite. He received a Knighthood, January 1925.

Courtesy of the Lancashire Constabulary

A week later in a letter to the Chief Constable of Lancashire County Police, Dr Wilson wrote asking for the meteorite to be returned or placed in some position where scientists may examine the rare find. He said that Professor Jenkins of the Godlee Observatory in Manchester, has been greatly interested in the meteorite, and was one of the first authorities to offer the explanation that the "airship" was in fact a meteorite.

Professor Jenkins was director of the Godlee Observatory and employed by the Manchester Technical School. The Godlee Observatory is situated in the centre of Manchester, and was gifted to the City of Manchester in 1903 by Francis Godlee who was a successful businessman in the cotton manufacturing industry.

Dr Wilson went on to say in his letter that an exhibition of the meteorite would allay fears still entertained by some that it was a German Zeppelin on a bombing raid.

LEFT
Francis Godlee.

Courtesy of 'Godlee Observatory, Manchester Astronomical Society'

In actual fact a piece of the meteorite which had been detached from the larger mass was put on display in the window of a grocer and drapers shop on Appley Lane North in Appley Bridge, the shop was owned by Mr James Rigby and visitors were able to see the meteorite and view it under a microscope or magnifying glass which had been set up. Coincidentally, when I moved to Appley Bridge in the early 1990s I lived next door to the house which was originally the village shop where the meteorite was displayed.

Dr Wilson's letter to the Chief Constable obviously did the trick, as a week later the police did in fact release the meteorite as it is recorded that following correspondence between Dr Wilson and Professor Jenkins of the Godlee Observatory, Professor Jenkins informed him that the meteorite" has been delivered to him by the police for examination.

LEFT
Photo of Mr Rigby and the shop in Appley Bridge taken 1907 where a piece of the meteorite went on display.

Provided courtesy of Barbara and Brian McDonald

RIGHT
Photo of the shop taken in 1907, the landing site of the meteorite is less than one mile away by road.

Provided courtesy of Barbara and Brian McDonald

Whilst at Manchester the meteorite was examined by Dr. Prior, who was Keeper of the Minerals at the Natural History Department of the British Museum. His colleague at the British Museum, Mr L. Fletcher, M.A., F.R.S., who was Director of the of the Natural History Department, wrote a letter to the chief police constable of Lancashire confirming that it

RIGHT
Photo of the same property today.

© Russell Parry

was a genuine meteorite. The letter also stated that in fact it was the largest to fall in Great Britain for 120 years and he went on to say that Mr. Maxwell, Principal of the Manchester School of Technology had made an analytical examination of the meteorite, and that a report was expected.

William Frederick Denning, the astronomer who studied comets and meteors and a former president of the Liverpool Astronomical Society, had an article published in the November 5th 1914 issue of the publication *Nature*. This concluded that based on the information collected regarding the flight of the object, it came from azimuth 335° counted West from South. (Azimuth is means of calculating the angle measured clockwise around the horizon from the north, or south, to the object or the intersection of the object's vertical circle with the horizon). Denning also calculated the probable radiant, this is the point in the sky from which the object appeared to originate. He found the radiant to be 348° + 2° which was the western region of the constellation of Pisces.

LEFT
The site of the Manchester School of Technology today where the first analysis of the meteorite took place.

© Russell Parry

The meteorite was seen to travel from above Stoke on Trent, at this point it would have been approx 30 miles high in the Mesosphere section of the atmosphere where most meteors burn up.

The meteorite travelled from here to where it landed in Appley Bridge a distance of 49 miles travelling at a velocity calculated at the time to be 8 miles a second (12.8km per second), when I spoke to the Natural History Museum, they thought that this figure was on the slow side. The Smithsonian Institute in Washington D.C., also informed me that the average velocity of objects entering Earth's atmosphere is around 10 to 70 km per second. The Chelyabinsk meteorite which landed in

LEFT
William Frederick Denning.

© Royal Astronomical Society / Science Photo Library

Russia in 2013 was estimated to be travelling at approximately 17.5 km per second, that's 10.8 miles per second.

Denning's article went on to state the hole made by the meteorite on impact was at an angle of 37° and this correlates with the radiant calculated of 348°.

Several explosions were heard during the entry of the meteorite as you will read accounts of in the various newspaper articles of the time in the next chapter. As the First World War had recently started, these explosions obviously gave rise to the thought of a raid by enemy Zeppelins with descriptions of the sound of cannons and thunder. However the explosions were due to the meteor breaking up and releasing energy as it entered and travelled through the more dense atmosphere of the Earth as it hurtled towards the ground. The explosions and thunder like noises reported seemed to follow the trail back along the flight path. Windows were even reported to rattle due to the vibrations caused by the explosions.

The breaking up of the meteorite and release of energy as it entered the Earth's atmosphere would also cause the reported ball of fire, the yellow and blue colours and tail of the meteorite as it travelled across the sky. Observations reported at the time state the object lost its 'luminosity' at a considerable height indicating the slowing down of the meteorite and this slowing down is backed up by the fact that the meteorite only penetrated the earth to a depth of 18 inches.

Newspaper reports of the time recorded sightings of the meteorite from the Stoke on Trent area, over Cheshire, Greater Manchester and Lancashire with reports also noted as far away as Halifax and Macclesfield.

INTENSIVE EXAMINATION

The article by W F Denning in *Nature* was followed up by a letter written by William C Jenkins, (Professor Jenkins of The Godlee Observatory in Manchester) which was published in the January 7th 1915 edition.

Professor Jenkins confirmed the meteorite belonged to the aerolite or stony group of meteorites and also described the appearance of piezoglyphs (now called regmaglypts), these are often described as 'thumb prints' which are on the surface of meteorites. These are caused by the flow of air over the surface of the meteorite as it enters the atmosphere resulting in melting of the outer crust and the formation of these depressions on the surface.

Professor Jenkins also described the coating of the meteorite as being dark brown to black in colour and the interior of the meteorite being a light grey colour. He quoted the dimensions as being length 9.65 inches, depth 9.13 inches and a width or thickness of 6.62 inches.

He mentioned when the meteorite arrived at the Godlee Observatory in Manchester it was in two pieces and weighed a total of 28lbs 13oz and commented that some considerable portions had been broken away since its discovery. It is interesting to note that at the

LEFT
The Godlee Observatory in the centre of Manchester today.

© Russell Parry

time it was found, the weight of the meteorite was recorded at over 30lbs. So it appears that between finding the meteorite and its transfer to the observatory some pieces were probably taken as souvenirs of the event! Professor Jenkins also commented that portions of the meteorite could easily be broken off by the thumb and finger.

In the article he went on to describe the thin outer coating up to 2mm thick and the 'lines of movement' being pushed back from the direction of motion. He also linked the glowing trail of the meteorite to the heating of the meteorite through the air and liberating portions of the meteorite. He suggested that some portions of the meteorite had only been in contact with the air during its later stages of entry and noticed in these areas that flakes of the outer skin had been broken away and fragments split off at the time of the apparent burst in the air at an altitude of approximately 20 miles. After this point the meteorite would be losing heat rather than gaining heat.

He also commented on the fractured surface, which was described as grey with a glittering mass of white and yellow points. These on analysis were found to be pyrites, the pyrites was found to contain nickel, iron, olivine and enstatite in the following proportions:

- Pyritic and metallic matter 5.07%
- Enstatite 31.5%
- Olivine 63.43%

The analysis carried out by Mr Ezra Lobb Rhead of The Manchester College of Technology found the meteorite was composed of the following: Silica, Magnesia, Iron, Alumina, Sulphur, Nickel, Phosphorus, Soda potash, Chlorine and Lime.

Professor Jenkins also had another article published in a popular magazine of the time, *The English Mechanic and World of Science* in October 1914. The article read as follows:

"Part of the meteor which (rumoured to be an airship) caused such sensation throughout Lancashire and Cheshire the week before last has been found in a field in the Wigan district. The brilliance of the meteor was especially noted in the Douglas valley, and the "remnants" of a meteor have been found on the land of Mr. Eric Lyon, of Halliwell Farm, Appley Bridge. It is said to be very heavy for its size, and has the appearance of iron which has been much burned, and small fragments of it taken between the fingers and rubbed would crumble. On rubbing the outer soft crust off, veins of what looked like gold and silver were seen. Superintendent Kelly, of the Wigan County Police force, went over to the farm and took possession of the meteorite on behalf of Mr. H. H. Lane, the Chief Constable of Lancashire. Afterwards a small fragment which had been detached from the larger mass was put on view in a shop-window at Appley Bridge. Superintendent Kelly says the piece he took charge of weighs some 30lb. On the outside it is dark brown in colour like rusty iron, and is covered with a sort of burnt powder. Inside the colour is light grey, with spots of gold and bright-coloured metals. It was taken to Preston to the county police headquarters for investigation and examination. Dr: J. H. Wilson, the medical officer for the district, describes the meteorite as being like a 'large stone,' irregular in shape, and externally of a reddish colour, similar to the appearance of rusty iron or of iron drawn from a fire. It is also very friable, he says, and pieces can be broken from it by the fingers alone. Internally the prevailing colour is that of French grey, the material being of varying hardness, and some parts having the resemblance of lead."

In December 1914, the same publication also published a letter by A N Preston together with a photograph of the meteorite as follows:

"In view of the interest which has been evinced in the Wigan meteorite by Mr. Godden and other readers, I thought the enclosed photograph of this interesting object might be acceptable for reproduction in "Ours." It clearly shows the pitted surface, and its curious shape. Writing to Mr Lane, the chief constable of Lancashire, Mr L. Fletcher, M.A., F.R.S., Director of the Natural History Department of the British Museum, says that his colleague, Dr. Prior, Keeper of the Minerals, has been to Manchester and seen the meteorite. He says it is undoubtedly a genuine one, whereas nine hundred and ninety-nine out of a thousand sent to the museum for inspection are mere terrestrial products. I am told it is the largest known meteorite which has fallen in this country for 120 years. I understand that Mr. Maxwell, Principal of the Manchester School of Technology, has

made an analytical examination of the meteorite, and that a report is expected from him in due course. As soon as this is received I will endeavour to forward you a copy. Through the microscope the meteorite seems to be composed entirely of silicious material mixed with bright metal of the appearance of silver".

Professor Jenkins gave the result of his investigations before a meeting of the Manchester Literary and Philosophical Society on Tuesday 3rd November 1914.

The Manchester Literary and Philosophical Society was founded in 1781 and at the time was located on George Street in Manchester. Unfortunately the building was destroyed by fire as a result of bombing of the city during the Second World War.

I am pleased to say the Manchester Literary and Philosophical Society is still very much in existence and in the library archives there is still reference to the lecture as follows:

LEFT Photo of Manchester Literary and Philosophical Society on George Street in 1930.

Reproduced with the kind permission of the Manchester Literary and Philosophical Society

"A paper, entitled "Some Notes on Aerolites. The Appley Bridge Aerolite of October 13th, 1914," was read by Mr. W. C. Jenkins, F.R.A.S., and Mr. E. L. Rhead, M.Sc.Tech., F.I.C. This paper will be printed in full in the Memoirs."

Unfortunately, the actual printed paper is no longer available or it was decided not to include it in the memoirs. We do know that at the lecture the meteorite was also available on display. Newspaper reports of the lecture stated that Professor Jenkins said:

"It could be safely assumed that this body was freely moving in space, and, approaching the earth was attracted by this larger mass, and so drew to itself the resistance offered by the atmosphere to its free passage, heating the surface in such a way as to round off corners. The time taken to pass through the earth's atmosphere was only a few seconds, so that the frictionary effect was enormous, rendering the surface of the aerolite white hot, and fusing the metals which it contained. Soon after the appearance of the aerolite a violent explosion was heard throughout Lancashire, Cheshire, and the surrounding counties. This evidently took place while the meteor was about 20 miles above the earth's surface. The results of the explosion were evident on the mass, and it was yet hoped to find other portions of the aerolite. The observations of the flight showed that when over the region

of Stoke-on-Trent the aerolite was at an altitude of about 29 miles, and fell along a line of 49 miles to a point 20 miles west of Manchester. The weight of this body, which was 28lbs 13oz, showed it to be the largest found in England for 120 years. The nearest approach to it within that period was the aerolite which fell in Shropshire in 1876 and weighed 7¾lbs. In the present case there was evidence that two or three pounds were missing. There were indications that the aerolite was of cometary origin and its composition was of the usual meteoric nature".

Mr E L Rhead of The Manchester College of Technology, who also presented the paper, was employed by the Manchester College of Technology and it was he who carried out the first analysis of the meteorite.

The presentation was the basis of another article which was published in the *Monthly Notices of the Royal Astronomical Society* in December 1914. This was a very detailed account and description by Mr. W. C. Jenkins and Mr. E. L. Rhead.

The article referred to the County Police removing the meteorite and then releasing it for examination and the article also made reference to the "manner in which it had been treated during the week between its fall and reaching the Godlee Observatory" as there was a significant weight difference between the find and when received for analysis. They were obviously not impressed!

RIGHT Inside the library of the Manchester Literary and Philosophical Society where the results of Professor Jenkins investigations were presented and the meteorite displayed. This photograph was taken in January 1921 showing the first Young Persons lecture.

The article described the "pyramidal form" and the detached piece of considerable size which accompanied the main body. The fractured surface and the surface of the detached piece was described as polished 'slikenside' surfaces with a more or less metallic appearance due to the amount of pyrites in the mass. Slikenside is a geological term usually describing the polishing effect and striations caused by a fault slip, in this case it was due to the force of the impact on the ground at a sideways angle.

A MOST EXCELLENT EXAMPLE

The exterior of the meteorite was described as "a most excellent example" with the dark brown to dark black skin or cortex ranging in thickness from that of 1.8mm to a film like skin and having a rough texture in some places and smooth in others. The article goes on to describe how the passage of the meteorite through the atmosphere has an effect on the surface, with the liquid surface being pushed by friction to the back of the mass and forming a distinct edge, described in the article as 'like a knife edge which has been melted and is irregular in outline'.

The article described "pit like depressions or thumb like depressions also known as piezoglyph" (now known as regmaglypts) and went on to state that these were formed as the meteorite entered the Earth's atmosphere, with the air flow and melting of the surface resulting in the thumb like depressions. The authors also came up with a theory that the regmaglypts as we call them today may have been formed by the combustion of sulphur and oxidation of the iron in the pyrites in the mass which is more readily removed by combustion. The theory went on to state 'the oxide of iron would at the temperature of the cortex form with other silicates and produce a fusable mixture resulting in the varying thickness of the outer coating and the development of the pits'.

The article stated the mass would not have been at a high temperature when it struck the ground. The mass was also travelling at low speed on the latter part of its entry flight as indicated by the shallow depth of penetration when it landed. The specific gravity analysis carried out on a detached fragment was calculated to be 3.336 and this tied up with the theoretical calculation from the composition of the meteorite.

The article also described the surface as viewed using a hand lens as being "a light ashy-grey colour and a perfectly granulated texture" and no perfectly formed chondrules.

The macrological appearance was stated as consisting of olivine, a magnesium iron silicate and enstatite, a magnesium silicate together with other silicates.

The olivine was described in the article as pale yellowish-green and in places well crystalised, the enstatite a whitish or grey or faintly coloured and the article went on to state, the fracture displays pyritic material which is mostly pyrrhotitic and troilitic and strongly magnetic. Pyrrhotite is an unusual iron-sulphide mineral and troilite is also a rare iron-sulphide mineral that mainly occurs in meteorites. The article also went on to state: "Small amounts of metallic iron were also present as fine particles and irregular flakes distributed through the mass which was soft and malleable." The iron flakes were described "rolled up into little cylinders of almost perfect form" when samples were taken and ground in a pestle. These again were strongly magnetic.

From analysis of the sample, the amount of pyritical matter was calculated as 5.07% this was based on a calculation from the percentage of sulphur found.

Nickel, Chlorides, Sodium and Phosphorus were also identified and being present. Antimony and Lead in trace amounts were also suspected. A "faint appearance of Strontium" was also observed.

The final section of the publication gave the following results of their analysis and a breakdown of the chemical composition:

The proportion of minerals	
Pyritic and metallic matter	5.07%
Enstatite	31.5%
Olivine	63.43%

Chemical composition	
Silica	39.7%
Iron	20.72%
Nickel	1.3%
Oxygen *to combine with excess Fe and Ni. After deducting sufficient to combine with S present*	5.25%
Magnesia	23.64%
Lime	Traces
Phosphorus	0.23%
Sulphur	1.84%
Alumina	6.2%
Soda, potash, chlorine etc by difference	1.12%

Following the newspaper articles of the time and publications in scientific literature over the months after the meteorite fall, there does not appear to be any further publications on the meteorite. However, from the 1960s onwards various articles on the description, analysis and properties of the meteorite have been published (see further reading section at the end of this book).

I thought that after the analysis the meteorite went straight into the hands of the museum in Manchester, but it appears that the meteorite was returned to Mr Lyon of Halliwell Farm. As it landed on his property, he was after all, the rightful owner of the meteorite.

TO THE NATURAL HISTORY MUSEUM IN LONDON

The Register of Meteorites at the Natural History Museum in London details the acquisition of the meteorite.

The first entry for the Appley Bridge meteorite under reference number 1919, 98 states:

'Meteoric stone fragments, weighing 3.003 grams, from the 33lb mass which fell on 13 October 1914 at Halliwell Farm, Appley Bridge.

The register also states where it was received from, which was the 'Municipal School of Technology by presentation 26 April 1919' (The fragments were sent for the preparation of micro section).

The next entry in the register was the purchase of the main mass and broken fragment of the meteorite from Mr Lyon. The entry states:

1920,40
Meteoric stone.
An almost complete stone measuring 25 x 17 x 16cm, and weighing 10900grams (24lbs 0 ¼oz), which fell on 13 October 1914 at Halliwell Farm, Appley Bridge, 4 miles WNW of Wigan Lancashire.

The next entry is:

1920,41
Meteoric stone, a partly crusted fragment weighing 1900grams (4lbs 3¼ozs) broken from (and fitting to the broken surface of) the above stone which fell on 13 October 1914 at Halliwell Farm, Appley Bridge, 4 miles WNW of Wigan Lancashire.

The next column against these two entries in the register states:

Mr Eric Lyon of Halliwell Farm Appley Bridge by purchase 24th January 1920.

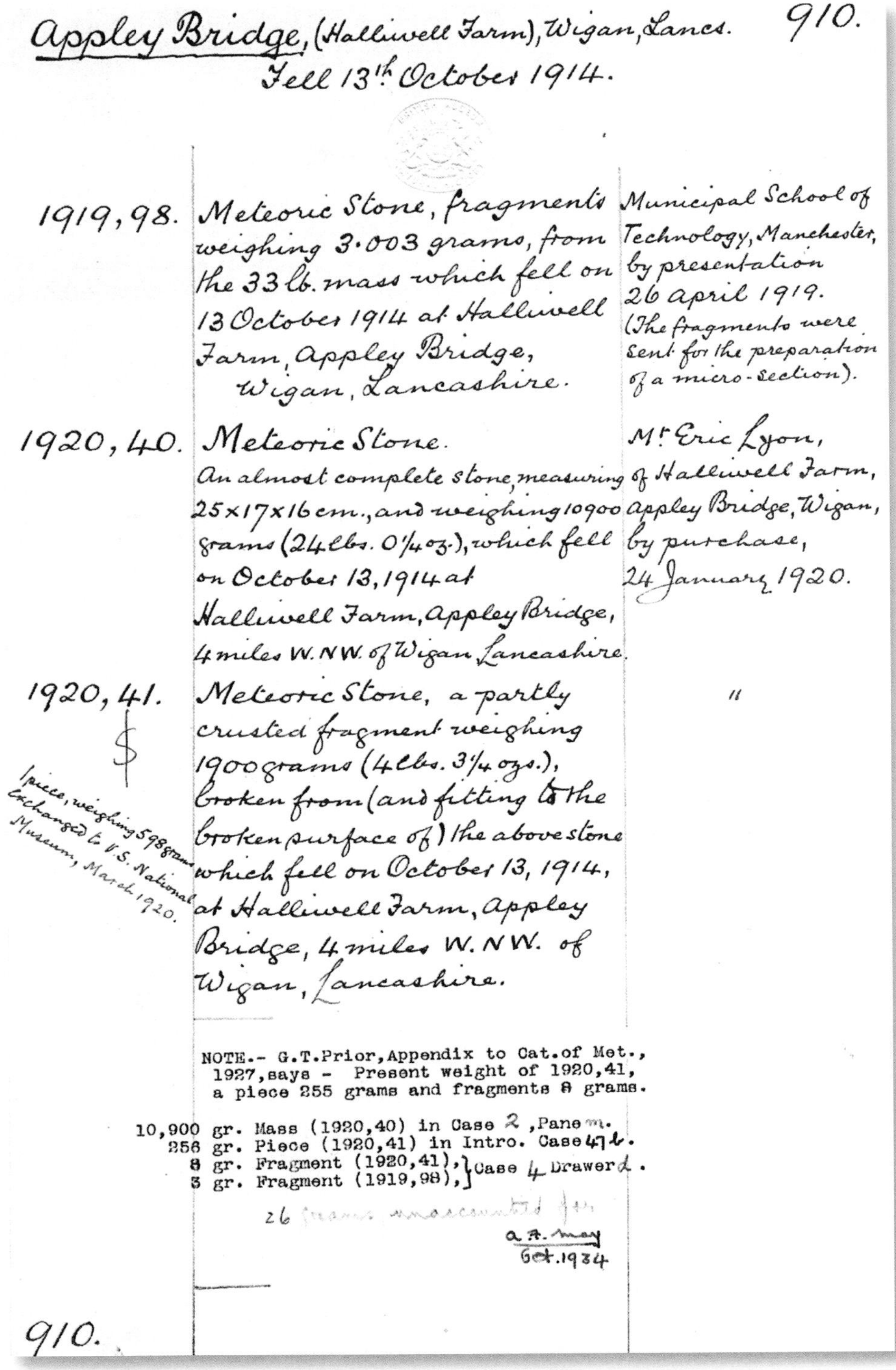

Appley Bridge, (Halliwell Farm), Wigan, Lancs. 910.
Fell 13th October 1914.

1919, 98.	Meteoric Stone, fragments weighing 3·003 grams, from the 33 lb. mass which fell on 13 October 1914 at Halliwell Farm, Appley Bridge, Wigan, Lancashire.	Municipal School of Technology, Manchester, by presentation 26 April 1919. (The fragments were sent for the preparation of a micro-section).
1920, 40.	Meteoric Stone. An almost complete stone, measuring 25×17×16 cm., and weighing 10900 grams (24 lbs. 0¼ oz.), which fell on October 13, 1914 at Halliwell Farm, Appley Bridge, 4 miles W.NW. of Wigan, Lancashire.	Mr Eric Lyon, of Halliwell Farm, Appley Bridge, Wigan, by purchase, 24 January 1920.
1920, 41. $	Meteoric Stone, a partly crusted fragment weighing 1900 grams (4 lbs. 3¼ ozs.), broken from (and fitting to the broken surface of) the above stone which fell on October 13, 1914, at Halliwell Farm, Appley Bridge, 4 miles W.NW. of Wigan, Lancashire.	"

1 piece, weighing 598 grams exchanged to U.S. National Museum, March 1920.

NOTE.- G.T.Prior, Appendix to Cat.of Met., 1927, says - Present weight of 1920,41, a piece 255 grams and fragments 8 grams.

10,900 gr. Mass (1920,40) in Case 2, Pane m.
256 gr. Piece (1920,41) in Intro. Case 47 b.
8 gr. Fragment (1920,41), } Case 4 Drawer d.
3 gr. Fragment (1919,98), }

26 grams unaccounted for
A. A. May
Oct. 1934

910.

RIGHT
The entry for the Appley Bridge meteorite in the Register of Meteorites.

Kindly provided by permission of the Trustees of the Natural History Museum

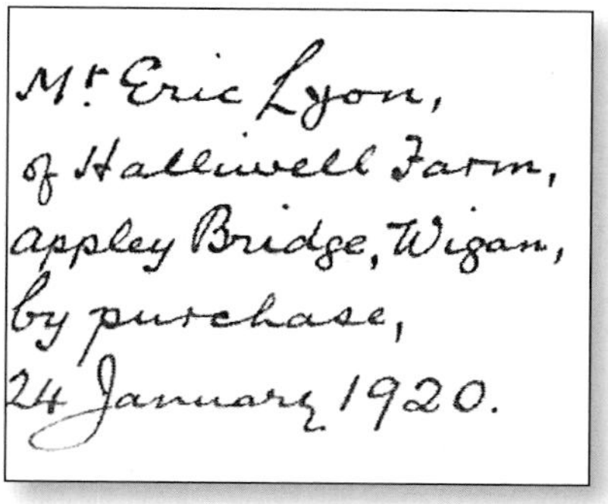

Mr Eric Lyon,
of Halliwell Farm,
appley Bridge, Wigan,
by purchase,
24 January 1920.

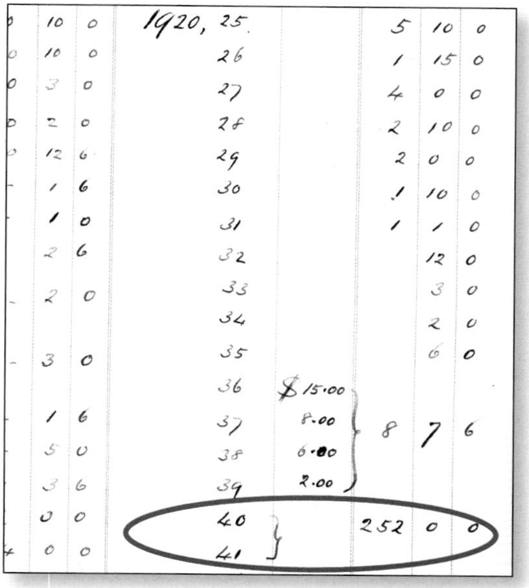

10	0	1920, 25		5	10	0
10	0	26		1	15	0
3	0	27		4	0	0
2	0	28		2	10	0
12	6	29		2	0	0
1	6	30		1	10	0
1	0	31		1	1	0
2	6	32			12	0
2	0	33			3	0
		34			2	0
3	0	35			6	0
		36	$15.00			
1	6	37	8.00	8	7	6
5	0	38	6.00			
3	6	39	2.00			
0	0	40		252	0	0
0	0	41				

TOP LEFT
Close up of the opposite entry for 1920,40 stating it was 'purchased' from Mr Lyon.

TOP RIGHT
Photograph of Mineralogy Register showing payment of £252 for the Appley Bridge meteorite 1920,40 and 1920,41.

Both images kindly provided by permission of the Trustees of the Natural History Museum

The sum paid to Mr Lyon for the meteorite in 1920 was £252. This, at the time, was a sizeable sum and would be the equivalent of around £10,000 today – £252 would have been enough to purchase a new Model T Ford back in 1920.

So, 6 years after the meteorite fall, Mr Lyon decided to sell the meteorite, perhaps he needed the money, perhaps it was just gathering dust or maybe just wanted other people to have the opportunity to see the famous meteorite.

COMING TO AMERICA

You can also see there is a note in the margin of this register stating '1 piece, weighing 598 grams exchanged to U.S. National Museum, March 1920'. This is otherwise known as the Smithsonian National Museum of Natural History which is in Washington D.C.

On researching the location of this specimen of the Appley Bridge meteorite the Smithsonian National Museum of Natural History were able to confirm the 'exchange' regarding the meteorite and provided me with a hand written note and typed letter dated April 8th 1920 from George Thurland Prior who was Keeper of Minerals at the British Museum to Professor George Merrill of the National Museum of Natural History in Washington, D. C. These are reproduced on page 28.

The piece of the Appley Bridge meteorite was exchanged with two other meteorites (Mornans and Ogi) for two pieces of the Cumberland Falls Meteorite which fell in Kentucky the previous year, 9th April 1919.

As you will see from the letter the Mornans meteorite, a meteorite fall in Drone, France, September 1875 and Ogi another meteorite fall from Kyushu, Japan 8th June 1741, were 'thrown in' as George T Prior put it, as the Appley Bridge specimen was 'not of so interesting a type'.

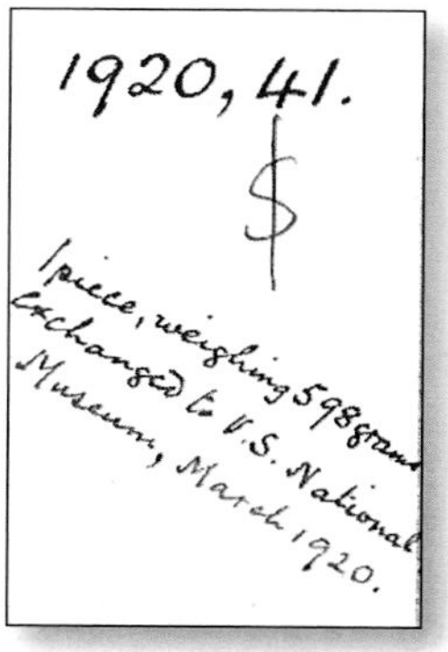

1920, 41.
$
1 piece, weighing 598 grams
Exchanged to U.S. National
Museum, March 1920.

LEFT
Close up of the note of exchange with the Smithsonian National Museum of Natural History.

Kindly provided by permission of the Trustees of the Natural History Museum

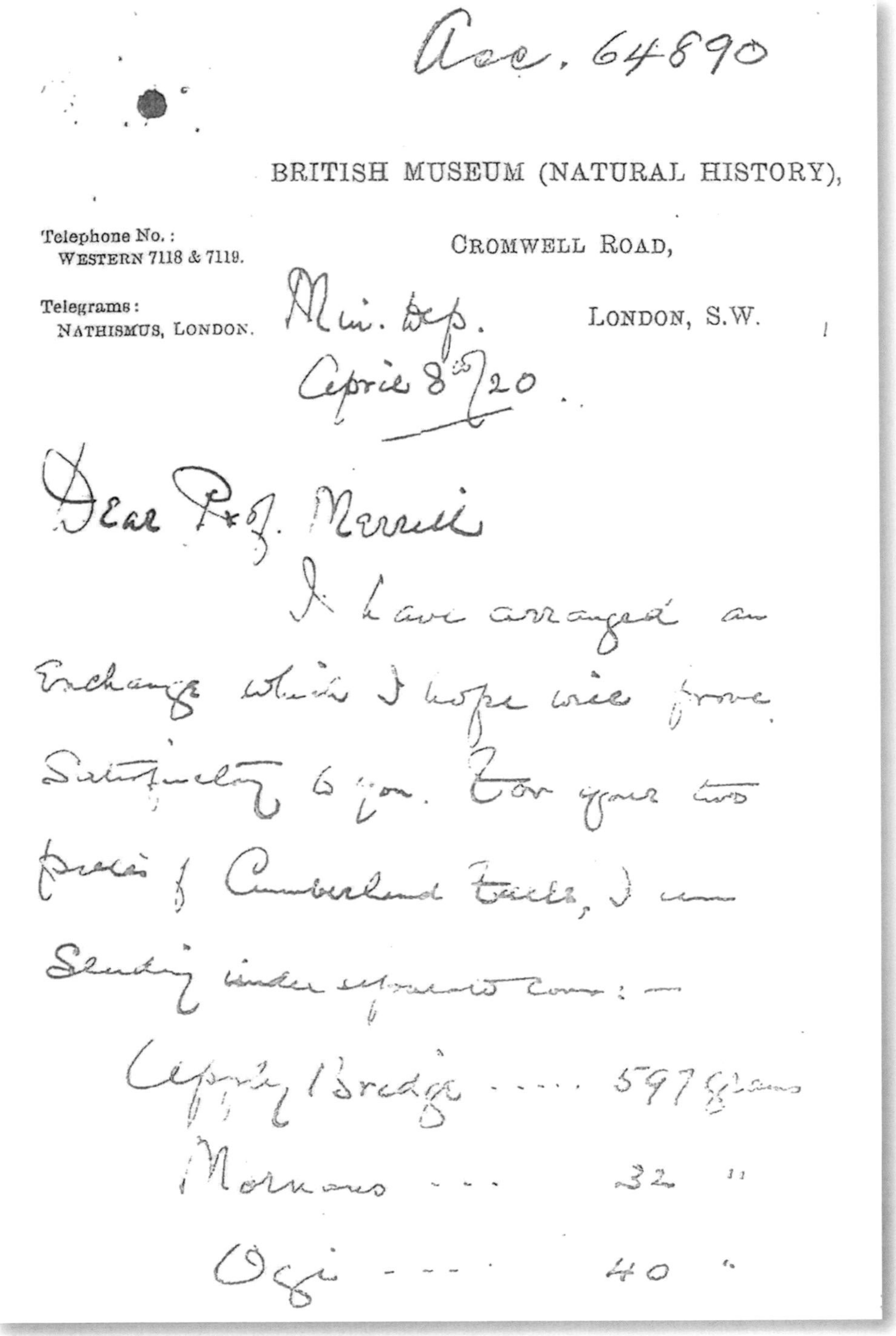

Acc. 64890

BRITISH MUSEUM (NATURAL HISTORY),

Telephone No.:
WESTERN 7118 & 7119.

CROMWELL ROAD,

Telegrams:
NATHISMUS, LONDON.

Min. Dep.

LONDON, S.W.

April 8th/20

Dear Prof. Merrill

I have arranged an exchange which I hope will prove satisfactory to you. For your two pieces of Cumberland Falls, I am sending under separate cover:—

Appley Bridge .... 597 grams
Mornans ... 32 "
Ogi ... 40 "

RIGHT
The hand written letter from George Thurland Prior of the British Museum (Natural History) to Professor George Merrill of the National Museum of Natural History in Washington, D. C. regarding the exchange of meteorites.

Provided courtesy of the Smithsonian Institution

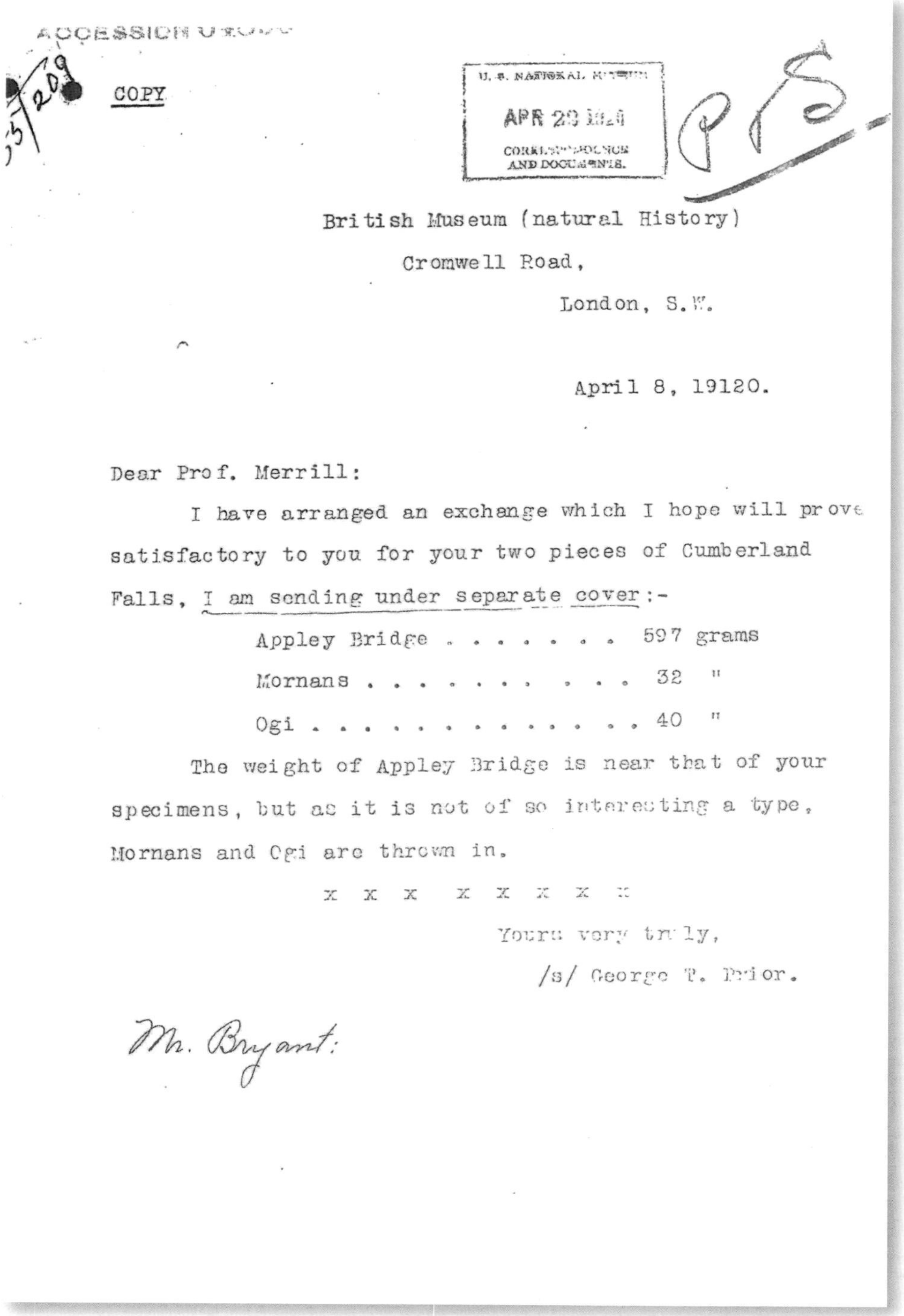

ACCESSION

COPY

APR 29 1920

CORRESPONDENCE AND DOCUMENTS.

British Museum (natural History)

Cromwell Road,

London, S.W.

April 8, 19120.

Dear Prof. Merrill:

I have arranged an exchange which I hope will prove satisfactory to you for your two pieces of Cumberland Falls, I am sending under separate cover:-

Appley Bridge	597 grams
Mornans	32 "
Ogi	40 "

The weight of Appley Bridge is near that of your specimens, but as it is not of so interesting a type, Mornans and Ogi are thrown in.

x x x x x x x x

Yours very truly,

/s/ George T. Prior.

Mr. Bryant:

LEFT
Typed version of the hand written note.

Provided courtesy of the Smithsonian Institution

3

CHAPTER 3

Newspaper accounts of the time

I must express my gratitude to the staff at Wigan Local Studies based at the Museum for Wigan Life where over the years I have spent many hours researching the newspaper archives for accounts of the meteorite fall.

THE FOLLOWING transcripts are from local newspaper articles and reveal the accounts of observations of the meteorite fall and of the activities following the finding of the meteorite. News of the Appley Bridge meteorite spread further afield, even to Australia, with the final transcript in this chapter from the Adelaide-based newspaper *The Advertiser*.

METEOR OVER CHESHIRE
A RUMOUR AND HOW IT AROSE

THE MANCHESTER GUARDIAN. THURSDAY, OCTOBER 15, 1914.

About nine o'clock on Tuesday night there was a rumour in several of the Cheshire suburbs of Manchester that an aeroplane, or something worse even than an aeroplane, had passed rapidly overhead. The thing seen was a travelling illumination in the sky, and there was an explosion. Many whose minds are "Zeppelin-proof" and who thought little or nothing of the illumination – knowing how many are the causes to account for such a thing – gave in to the explosion, and it appeared consequently that an aeroplane was passing over peaceful Cheshire, distributing bombs.

The circumstances were obligingly made known to the "Manchester Guardian" over the telephone by several people who had seen the visitor. Careful enquiry was made of country police who were likely to have their attention called to such a thing, but without any corroboration being obtained, until from a police office in the track of the trouble it was reported that there had been no aeroplane, but in point of fact a short though lively thunderstorm. This seemed to account for the more alarming rumour, and, though not quite an accurate explanation, it was true to the extent that the disturbance was atmospheric.

The trouble seems to have been caused by a meteor, and the noise was due, we are informed, to the explosion of the meteor. It appears that the earth has lately been meeting many meteors. They come at a time when they are peculiarly liable to be misunderstood.

Provided courtesy of Wigan Archives & Local Studies WLCT

KNUTSFORD DIVISION GUARDIAN.
FRIDAY, OCTOBER 16, 1914.

AIRSHIP SCARE
SKY FLASH AND EXPLOSION
THE ALARM OF WAR
SCIENTISTS EXPLANATION

A scare was caused over a wide area of Cheshire shortly before nine o'clock on Tuesday evening by a bright passage of light across the sky followed by an explosion. It was at once conjectured by many people that a war airship had passed over the country and dropped a bomb. An astonishing amount of evidence in support of this theory was given the following day by people from almost every part of the country, and the alarming visitation was the one topic of conversation.

Mr Jenkins, of the Godlee Observatory, Manchester has provided a rational explanation of the occurrence. The illumination, he states, was caused by a meteor exploding. Some exceptionally brilliant meteors have been seen of late, Mr Jenkins mentions, and explosions have on two occasions marked their disappearance. It is only the larger meteors which come to so noisy an end.

Provided courtesy of The Knutsford Division Guardian 1914, as held at Knutsford Library

KNUTSFORD DIVISION GUARDIAN.
FRIDAY, OCTOBER 16, 1914.

BY THE WAY

The suggestion than an airship hovered over the district on Tuesday night was quickly accepted as true. Unfortunately many good people had a restless night in consequence.

Provided courtesy of The Knutsford Division Guardian 1914, as held at Knutsford Library

THE WIGAN OBSERVER AND DISTRICT ADVERTISER.
SATURDAY OCTOBER 17, 1914.

AGITATION AT GOLBORNE

Our Golborne representative writes that considerable agitation was displayed in Golborne on Tuesday evening about 9.30 by what was thought to be an airship flying over the township. It appeared like a shooting star but there was a variation of lights. The airship moved towards Warrington. At one point there seemed to be an explosion which was distinctly heard and lights were made visible to the residents of Golborne and Lowton. The appearance had been the subject of much conversation over the following days.

Provided courtesy of Wigan Archives & Local Studies WLCT

3

AIRSHIP OR METEOR?

BRILLIANT OBJECT IN THE SKY NOISE LIKE DISTANT CANNONADING

THE WIGAN EXAMINER. SATURDAY, OCTOBER 17, 1914.

A great many people in this district were startled on Tuesday evening by the appearance in the sky of a brilliant light – some averred it was that of an airship – which flashed past and disappeared in a few seconds. It came from a southerly direction and is reported to have been observed in Cheshire and the Manchester districts, and was seen by hundreds in Wigan and Horwich. What, however, was imagined to be an airship was doubtless a meteor which sometimes make their appearance at this period of the year. A representative of the "Examiner" who was in the Gidlow district about a quarter to nine in the evening was suddenly startled by a vivid flash as if electricity, which lighted up the whole place.

On turning around and looking in the sky he observed what seemed to be a ball of fire, with a tail attached, travelling at terrific speed in a northerly direction. The object however vanished from sight so quickly that there was not time to see it sufficiently to give an adequate description. After the disappearance of the meteor there was for about a couple of minutes a rumbling noise as of canons being fired miles away, or of distant thunder. There would seem to be little doubt that the object seen was a meteor.

The most remarkable meteors are those which are followed by the falling of stones to the earth. A ball of fire crosses the sky so bright as to be visible, if it appears in the daytime, sometimes even at hundreds of miles from the meteor and if it appears at night it is bright enough to light up the whole landscape. It transverses the sky, generally finishing its course in a few seconds. It suddenly goes out, either with or without an apparent bursting in pieces and after a short period a loud detonation heard in all the region near the place where the meteor had disappeared.

A meteor that was seen in December 1876 by persons in the State of Kansas, was described as a bright fireball rising from near where the moon was in the Western sky. It increased in brilliancy as it proceeded, and became so bright as to compel the attention of everyone out of doors. For four or five minutes afterwards there were loud explosions like distant cannonading or thunder, or like the rattling of empty wagons over stony roads.

Probably the appearance of the meteor was responsible for the singular rumour that was circulated with regard to the camp at Winstanley – that a bomb had been thrown from an aeroplane on to the camp.

OBSERVATORY CURATOR'S OPINION

Since we wrote the above, Mr Jenkins, Curator of the Godlee Observatory, Manchester, has given his opinion on the subject. He states that the illumination was caused by a meteor, and that the loud report was due to the meteor exploding. "Some exceptionally brilliant meteors have been seen of late" adds Mr Jenkins "and on two occasions their disappearance have been followed by explosions. The meteors occasionally, if small, burn out early in their visible trail, but if they are large, the heating causes a sort of explosive rupture of the mass which gives the report such as that which was heard on Tuesday evening.

A Swinton correspondent writes as follows on the subject:- "So quickly did the thing transverse the sky and in such a way was it lit up, that it could be nothing else but a meteor. To the naked eye the whole thing did not appear to be more than two feet in length and one foot in breadth. It was all fire, and how anyone could imagine it to be an airship passes my comprehension as I have not yet heard of Zeppelins or other aircraft sailing through the air at a speed of thousands of miles per second, lit up stem to stern."

SEEN IN THE DISTRICTS

The meteor was seen in all the out-townships round Wigan, but most of the inhabitants appear to believe that the object was an airship. Appley Bridge people are absolutely convinced that it was an airship as they "heard the buzzing of the engine."

Our Golborne correspondent states that considerable agitation was caused at Golborne on Tuesday evening by "what was thought to be an airship flying over the township." It appeared "like a shooting star, but there was a variation of lights." At one period there seemed to be an explosion, which was distantly heard and lights made visible to residents in Golborne and Lowton.

Provided courtesy of Wigan Archives & Local Studies WLCT

METEOR OR AIRSHIP

EXCITEMENT IN THE DISTRICT

THE WIGAN OBSERVER AND DISTRICT ADVERTISER. SATURDAY OCTOBER 17, 1914.

On Tuesday night many people of Wigan and district averred that they saw an airship in the skies
It was brilliantly illuminated they said with a yellow light at one end and blue light at the other. Reports as to explosions were heard.
Certain it is that numerous persons connected the sight in the heavens with the visitation of a hostile airship. Seen from Wigan Lane, Gidlow Lane and many places in the out-districts to former a fruitful source of comment and conversation. Alarm was manifested in several instances especially when it became bruited about that a searchlight was used.
No reports have been received, however, of any aircraft manoeuvring in these parts, and scientific men have come forward with a solution of the mystery. The explanation is that a meteor had flashed across the sky, and this supposition is confirmed by astronomical experts who state that the description of the mysterious light and the noise of the explosion tallies with a meteoric visitation which might occur at this time of the year.
Mr Jenkins of the Godlee Observatory in Manchester has provided this explanation of the occurrence. The illumination, he stated, was caused by a meteor and the loud report was due to the meteor exploding. Some exceptionally brilliant meteors had been seen of late, Mr Jenkins mentioned, and explosions have on two occasions marked their disappearance, it is only large meteors which come to a noisy end.

Provided courtesy of Wigan Archives & Local Studies WLCT

3

THE ZEPPELIN SCARE AT WIGAN

MYSTERIOUS "AIRSHIP" DISCOVERED
CLAIMED BY THE COUNTY POLICE
INTERESTING DESCRIPTION

THE WIGAN EXAMINER. TUESDAY, OCTOBER 20, 1914.

On Tuesday evening last week Lancashire and Cheshire, and of course, Wigan, were agog by the reported visit of an enemy Zeppelin, which scared the more nervous population into belief that we were being attacked from the skies by the Germans.

The newspaper the next morning gave considerable space to a discussion of the strange object which, by its brilliance, had certainly called for more than passing notice. Many could not be convinced that the astral visitor was a meteorite, but we think that after subsequent discoveries they may rest satisfied on that point.

On Wednesday morning two gentlemen were out shooting on the farm of Mr Edward Lyon at Appley Bridge , when they came across what at first sight appeared to be a hare in the grass. As the sportsmen approached, the object of their attention did not move, and it was found that the "hare" was a hole in the ground. As in the opinion of many people the meteorite dropped in the Douglas Valley the night previously, the sportsmen examined the place very carefully, and in the hole, which measured two feet square by about the same depth, discovered a reddish mass. They obtained a spade, dug the thing out, and had it conveyed to the farmhouse.

The same day Dr Wilson of Standish, who is in attendance at Mr Lyon's house inspected the interesting curiosity. He has examined it twice and he supplies us with the following description: The mass is just like a large stone, irregular in shape, and externally of a reddish colour similar to the appearance of rusty iron, or of iron drawn from a fire. It is also very friable he says, and pieces can be broken from it by the fingers alone. Internally the prevailing colour is that of French grey, the material is of varying hardness, and some parts having the resemblance of lead. It is about 30 inches in circumference and weighs about 30lbs. When it was taken from the hole several pieces were accidentally broken off it. In the meantime an officer from the County Police has visited Mr Lyon's farm and removed the meteorite in a motor car. On Monday Dr Wilson wrote to the Chief Constable of the County (Mr H H Lane) asking that the curiosity might be returned or placed in some position where scientists may examine the rare find. He adds that Professor Jenkins of the Manchester Observatory, has been greatly interested in the meteorite, and was one of the first authorities to offer the explanation that the "airship" was a meteor. Dr Wilson also thinks that its exhibition would allay fears still entertained by some that last week's illumination was in reality a German Zeppelin.

Provided courtesy of Wigan Archives & Local Studies WLCT

THE AERIAL SENSATION
THE MYSTERY SAID TO BE CLEARED UP

THE WIGAN OBSERVER AND DISTRICT ADVERTISER. TUESDAY, OCTOBER 20, 1914.

The "airship" mystery which caused such a sensation throughout Lancashire and Cheshire last week, it has been reported cleared up by the finding in a field at Appley Bridge of a curious reddish mass 2ft 6in in circumference in a hole 18inches deep. This is the meteorite which dropped and buried itself in the ground at the farm of Mr E Lyon. It is irregular in character and is the colour of rusty iron, or of iron which has been withdrawn from a fire. It weighed about 30lbs. It has been removed by a Police officer, but efforts are being made to have it returned as an object of much interest to scientists.

Provided courtesy of Wigan Archives & Local Studies WLCT

IS IT THE METEOR? DISCOVERY IN A FIELD NEAR WIGAN

KNUTSFORD DIVISION GUARDIAN. TUESDAY, OCTOBER 20, 1914

The mysterious explosion which was heard in various parts of Lancashire and Cheshire on Tuesday night of last week has had an interesting sequel.

"Guardian" readers will recollect that the phenomenon was attributed to the explosion of a meteor. It is now announced that portions of a meteorite have been found at Appley Bridge near Wigan, on a farm occupied by Mr E Lyon. Two sportsmen shooting over Mr Lyon's land noticed a hole in the ground 2ft square and 18in deep.

In the hole was a curious reddish mass which was later dug out and taken to the farm.

Dr Wilson of Standish states it is just like a stone, irregular in character, and is the colour of rusty iron, or of iron which has just been withdrawn from a fire. It was about two feet six inches in circumference and weighed about 30lbs. Professor Jenkins, curator of the Godlee Observatory, Manchester has been intensely interested in the discovery and he was the first to suggest that the brilliant visitor was a stray object from space which had come within the range of the earths atmosphere of gravitation.

Provided courtesy of The Knutsford Division Guardian 1914, as held at Knutsford Library

NOT AN AIRSHIP BUT A METEORITE

POLICE TAKE POSSESSION OF FALLEN BODY AT APPLEY BRIDGE

THE WIGAN OBSERVER AND DISTRICT ADVERTISER. SATURDAY, OCTOBER 24, 1914.

The airship mystery which caused such a sensation throughout Lancashire and Cheshire last week has been cleared up by the finding of a meteorite in a field in the Wigan district. There was great agitation in the Wigan district on Tuesday night last week when the luminous body was seen by many people. Next morning and for days afterwards there was talk about a mysterious airship and all sorts of rumours got abroad. It was generally noticed that the moving body in its swift transit across the heavens emitted what seemed to be explosions, and Professor Jenkins of the Manchester Corporations Godlee Observatory came forward next day with the suggestion that the brilliant visitor of the atmosphere was a stray object from space which had come within the range of the earths sphere of gravitation and gave a scientific explanation of exploding meteors. The brilliance of the mysterious object was especially noticed in the Douglas Valley, and this was explained the next day by the finding of the remnants of a meteor on the land of Mr Eric Lyon of Halliwell Farm Appley Bridge. An employee on the farm was out shooting on the day after the travelling light had been seen when he noticed what seemed to be a newly turned up mound in a field about 3 minutes walk from the farm buildings. Thinking the rabbits had been more than usually industrious he went and examined the place and was surprised to find a reddish mass of strange looking matter some two feet in diameter embedded in the ground. He reported his find to Mr Lyon who dug a piece of it out of its bed. He found the piece very heavy for its size, and noticed that it had the appearance of iron which had been much burned and small fragments of it taken between the fingers and rubbed would crumble. On rubbing the outer surface soft crust off, veins of mineral gold and silver in colour were seen. News got abroad of the discovery and Superintendent Kelly of the Wigan County Policy Force went over to the farm and took possession of the body on behalf of Mr H H Lane Chief Constable of Lancashire County.

Afterwards a small fragment which had been detached from the larger mass was put on view in the shop window of Mr James Rigby at Appley Bridge and was viewed by visitors under the microscope.

Superintendent Kelly of the Wigan County Police who took possession of the meteorite explains in an interview with the representative that the find entirely dispels the idea of an airship passing over the district. The fallen body he says weighs some 30lbs and is heavier than it looks. On the outside it is dark brown in colour like rust iron and is covered with a sort of burnt powder. Inside the colour is light grey with spots of gold and bright coloured metals. There is no doubt , the Superintendent adds, that it is a genuine meteorite and it was taken to Preston to the County Policy Headquarters for investigations and examination.

Dr J H Wilson, the medical officer for the district who had seen the meteorite told a representative that everybody who saw it during its fall to earth thought it was an airship and many people seeing the exploding matter would have it that it was a German Zeppelin carrying guns and discharging them during its nightly passage. The meteorite in its decent lighted up all the neighbourhood, and Dr Wilson, who has spoken to numerous residents in Appley Bridge says that many of them used the expression that although it was night they could see to pick up a pin by the light given out.

" It is rather remarkable" the Doctor says, "that an object of such comparatively small dimensions should give out such a great light because everybody is agreed as to the amount of light that it did give out". Dr Wilson, who examined the meteorite, describes it as being like a large stone , irregular in shape and externally of a reddish colour similar to the appearance of rusty iron, or of iron drawn from a fire. It is also very friable he says, and pieces can be broken from it by the fingers alone. Internally the prevailing colour is that of French grey, the materials being of varying hardness, and some parts having the resemblance of lead.

Its is stated that the body had dug itself into the earth in a slanting direction and this may help to explain why in falling it should give the impression of an airship travelling along.

The meteorite was broken into two pieces when found in the ground.

Dr Wilson of Standish has been corresponding with Professor Jenkins of Manchester, in regard to the discovery.

We never know where these things will drop said Professor Jenkins to a press representative. There have been several instances of similar masses reaching earth and being found. Many cases are on record where the mass weighed more than the one found at Appley Bridge. The largest known in recent years was at Antrim about 12 years ago. It fell during the harvest time and weighed about three times more than the present one. I have no knowledge of one having previously dropped in Lancashire. The mass was no doubt the main portion of the meteor which gave the visible flare and was the largest remnant which survived the explosion. It would be interesting to know if portions had been found in any other parts of the country.

Provided courtesy of Wigan Archives & Local Studies WLCT

THE WIGAN OBSERVER AND DISTRICT ADVERTISER. SATURDAY, OCTOBER 31, 1914.

THE APPLEY BRIDGE METEORITE BEING EXAMINED BY PROFESSOR JENKINS

Professor Jenkins of the Manchester Corporation's Godlee Observatory, has written to Dr J. H. Wilson of Standish, informing him that the meteorite which fell on the land of Mr Eric Lyon of Halliwell Farm, Appley Bridge, at the time of the sensation as to a mysterious "airship" passing over the district, as reported in last Saturday's "Observer" has been delivered to him by the police for examination. Dr Wilson understands that the results of Professor Jenkin's investigations will be made public in due course.

Provided courtesy of Wigan Archives & Local Studies WLCT

3

THE APPLEY BRIDGE METEORITE

LARGEST FOUND IN ENGLAND FOR 120 YEARS

THE WIGAN OBSERVER AND DISTRICT ADVERTISER. SATURDAY, NOVEMBER 7, 1914.

Mr W. C. Jenkins, the curator of the Godlee Observatory, Manchester, to whom the meteorite which fell at Appley Bridge on the 13th of last month was sent for examination, gave the result of his investigations before a meeting of the Manchester Literary and Philosophical Society on Tuesday night, when the fallen aerolite was on exhibition. He said it could be safely assumed that this body was freely moving in space, and, approaching the earth was attracted by this larger mass, and so drew to itself the resistance offered by the atmosphere to its free passage, heating the surface in such a way as to round off corners. The time taken to pass through the earth's atmosphere was only a few seconds, so that the frictionary effect was enormous, rendering the surface of the aerolite white hot, and fusing the metals which it contained. Soon after the appearance of the aerolite a violent explosion was heard throughout Lancashire, Cheshire, and the surrounding counties. This, Mr Jenkins said evidently took place while the meteor was about 20 miles above the earth's surface. The results of the explosion were evident on the mass, and it was yet hoped to find other portions of the aerolite. Mr Jenkins said the observations of the flight showed that when over the region of Stoke-on-Trent the aerolite was at an altitude of about 29 miles, and fell along a line of 49 miles to a point 20 miles west of Manchester. The weight of this body, which was 28lbs 13oz, showed it to be the largest found in England for 120 years. The nearest approach to it within that period was the aerolite which fell in Shropshire in 1876 and weighed 7¾lbs. In the present case there was evidence that two or three pounds were missing. There were indications that the aerolite was of cometary origin and its composition was of the usual meteoric nature.

Provided courtesy of Wigan Archives & Local Studies WLCT

A STARTLING METEOR

THE ADVERTISER (ADELAIDE, SOUTH AUSTRALIA). SATURDAY, JANUARY 2, 1915

Part of a meteor which (rumored to be an airship) caused such a sensation throughout Lancashire and Cheshire in October, has been found in a field in the Wigan district. The brilliance of the meteor was especially noted in the Douglas Valley, and this was explained next day by the finding of the remnants of a meteor on the land of Mr. Eric Lyon, of Halliwell Farm, Appley Bridge. An employee who was out shooting on the day after the travelling light had been seen noticed what seemed to be a newly-turned-up mound in a field about three minutes' walk from the farm buildings. Thinking the rabbits had been more than usually industrious he examined the place, and was surprised to find a reddish mass of strange-looking matter, some 2 ft. in diameter, embedded in the ground. He reported his find to Mr. Lyon, who dug a piece of it out of its bed. He found it very heavy for its size, and noticed that it had the appearance of iron which had been much burned, and small fragments of it taken between the fingers and rubbed would crumble. On rubbing the outer soft crust off veins of what looked like gold and silver were seen. Superintendent Kelly, of the Wigan County Police force, went over to the farm and took possession of the meteorite on behalf of Mr. H. H. Lane, the Chief Constable of Lancashire. Afterwards a small fragment which had been detached from the larger mass was put on view in a shop window at Appley Bridge.

Superintendent Kelly says the piece he look charge of weighs some 30 lb. On the outside it is dark brown in color, like rusty iron, and is covered with a sort of burnt powder. Inside the color is light grey, with spots of gold and bright-colored metals. It was taken to Preston to the county police headquarters for investigation and examination.

Dr. J. H. Wilson, the medical officer for the district, who has seen the meteorite, told a press representative that everybody who saw it during its fall to the earth thought it was an airship, and many people would have it that it was a German Zeppelin carrying guns and discharging them during its passage. He describes the meteorite as being like a large stone, irregular in shape, and externally of a reddish color, similar to the appearance of rusty iron, or of iron drawn from a fire. It is also very friable, he says and pieces can be broken from it by the fingers alone. Internally the prevailing color is that of French grey, the material being of varying hardness, and some parts having the resemblance of lead.

Provided courtesy of Trove Digitised Newspapers from http://nla.gov.au/nla.news-article5437671. Digitised by The National Library of Australia.

CHAPTER 4

Where is the Appley Bridge meteorite now?

As stated in an earlier chapter, the Appley Bridge meteorite was purchased from Mr Lyon on 24th January 1920 by the British Museum Natural History.

SINCE THEN sections of the meteorite have been exchanged or given away to various museums and institutions all around the world and it has been interesting to track down some of the specimens and their whereabouts. Of course there are many collectors of meteorites and quite often specimens become available for sale via websites and auctions and occasionally specimens of the Appley Bridge meteorite do come up for sale.

Following the acquisition of the meteorite by the British Museum Natural History, the first exchange was a 598 gram piece with the **United States National Museum of Natural History** in Washington, D.C. USA which was carried out in March 1920. In the earlier chapter you would have seen the letter of exchange between Keeper of Minerals at the British Museum, George Thurland Prior and Professor George Merrill of the National Museum of Natural History which is part of the Smithsonian Institution.

The Smithsonian

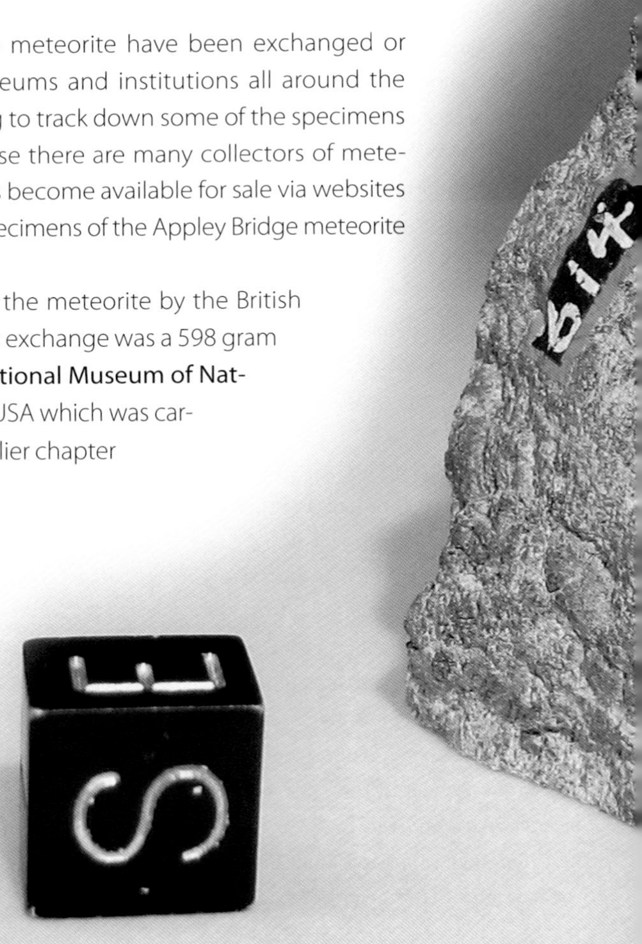

RIGHT The Appley Bridge meteorite at the Smithsonian Institute.

© Provided courtesy of the Smithsonian Institution

ABOVE
The Smithsonian Institute sample of the Appley Bridge meteorite showing crust.

Provided courtesy of the Smithsonian Institution

OPPOSITE
Smithsonian photomicrograph of the Appley Bridge meteorite (crossed-polars 2.5 x magnification).

Provided courtesy of the Smithsonian Institution

Institute (Natural History Museum) currently houses the largest meteorite collection in the world. The collection contains both historical specimens and specimens collected as part of the Antarctic meteorite collection program.

The Smithsonian were very helpful in my research in sending details of the exchange and in providing photographs of the Appley Bridge meteorite sample they have in their collection. They also took a photomicrograph of a section of the meteorite.

Photomicrographs are taken of a polished thin section of the meteorite, which is approximately 30μm (or 0.03mm) in thickness. Thin sections are mounted on glass slides, and when examined with a polarizing microscope, allow the determination of properties that are difficult (if not impossible) to determine with the naked eye, e.g. mineral identification, composition, textural relationships and rock-forming processes.

The colours that you see are called interference colours, and result from the way in which light interacts with the polarizer on the microscope. Different minerals can display different ranges of interference colours, so this gives us a useful tool for identification.

TOP RIGHT
Photo of the register at the Manchester Museum

Image courtesy of The Manchester Museum

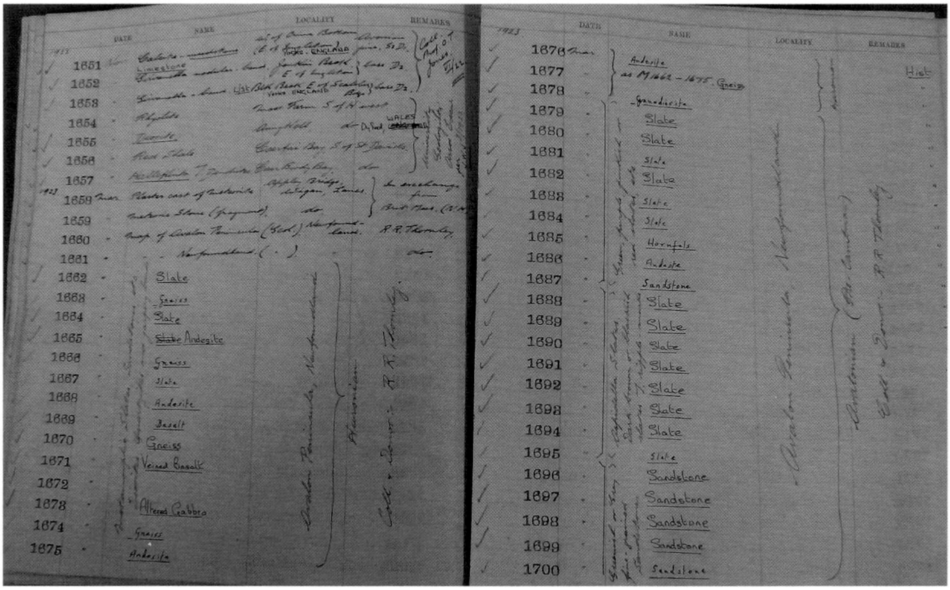

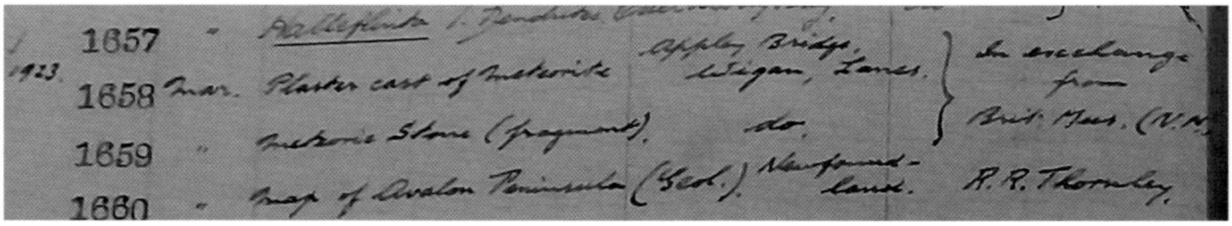

	1657	Hälleflinta		
1923.	1658 Mar.	Plaster cast of meteorite	Appley Bridge, Wigan, Lancs.	In exchange from Brit. Mus. (N.H.)
	1659 "	Meteoric Stone (fragment).	do.	
	1660 "	Map of Avalon Peninsula (Geol.)	Newfoundland.	R. R. Thornley.

CENTRE & BOTTOM RIGHT
Entry for the Appley Bridge plaster cast (1658) and actual fragment of the meteorite (1659).

Close up shows 'In exchange from the British Museum Natural History'

Images courtesy of The Manchester Museum

CHAPTER 5

My close encounter of the meteorite kind!

I travelled down to London on Sunday 3rd November 2013 to avoid any delays in getting there on the Monday morning which was when I had arranged to view the Appley Bridge meteorite at the Natural History Museum.

FINALLY, I was going to see and hopefully handle the meteorite I had read so much about over all the previous years. Getting up early on the Monday morning I left my hotel and travelled with the mass of morning commuters on the underground to South Kensington and then from there, the short walk to the Natural History Museum.

What an impressive building the Natural History Museum is, first opening in 1881 and home to some 70 million specimens, but I was just there to see one thing, the Appley Bridge meteorite.

Before my meeting with the Assistant Meteorite Curator, I took the opportunity to look at some the of the other meteorite exhibits on display. However, these were not all in one area, so I started at the Red Zone of the museum which had exhibits explaining the beginning of the universe and our solar system which included information on the formation of meteorites.

Then it was over to the old part of the museum to the Minerals collection where there were more meteorite exhibits and specimens of the various types and classifications of meteorites.

Then I went to the 'Vault' exhibition which housed a few more specimens including the famous 'diamond dust', minute particles of diamonds present in some meteorites, the diamond particles are thought to pre-date our own solar system.

THE ENCOUNTER BEGINS

I met the Assistant Meteorite Curator at the reception at the Exhibition Road entrance and we entered behind the scenes of this great museum and down into the basement where the Mineral & Planetary Sciences department is located.

We cleared a table on which we could view the meteorite and it was taken out of its storage box and protective covering.

For the first time I could see the actual meteorite and I just thought about all the people that had been involved in its discovery. The two gentlemen out shooting who found the meteorite; Mr Eric Lyon the landowner at Halliwell Farm; Dr J H Wilson the Medical Officer for the local district. Superintendent Kelly of Wigan County Police who collected the meteorite from Halliwell Farm; Chief Constable H H Lane of the Lancashire Police; Professor Jenkins curator of the Godlee Observatory; Dr Prior the Keeper of Minerals at the British Museum who was sent to see the meteorite in Manchester; and Mr James Rigby owner of the Appley Bridge shop where the meteorite was displayed for the locals to see.

RIGHT
The author with the main mass of the Appley Bridge meteorite.

Photographed by Deborah-Jayne Cassey Photograph of Appley Bridge meteorite BM.1920,40 by permission of the Trustees of the Natural History Museum.

Then of course I realised that this object in front of me had a much greater history, it had been travelling through space for 4.6 billion years from the beginning of our solar system.

Wearing protective gloves I was able to handle the meteorite and I was surprised by its weight, 'heavy for its size', exactly as described in the newspaper reports following the fall of the meteorite. The most striking features for me were the 'thumb prints' and the crust formed during the entry of the meteorite into the Earth's atmosphere.

LEFT
Close up of the surface of the Appley Bridge meteorite.

Photographed by Russell Parry Photograph of Appley Bridge meteorite BM.1920,40 by permission of the Trustees of the Natural History Museum.

LEFT
Cut surface of the meteorite.

Photograph of Appley Bridge meteorite BM.1920,40 by permission of the Trustees of the Natural History Museum.

5

RIGHT
Close up of meteorite surface.

Photographed by Russell Parry Photograph of Appley Bridge meteorite BM.1920,40 by permission of the Trustees of the Natural History Museum.

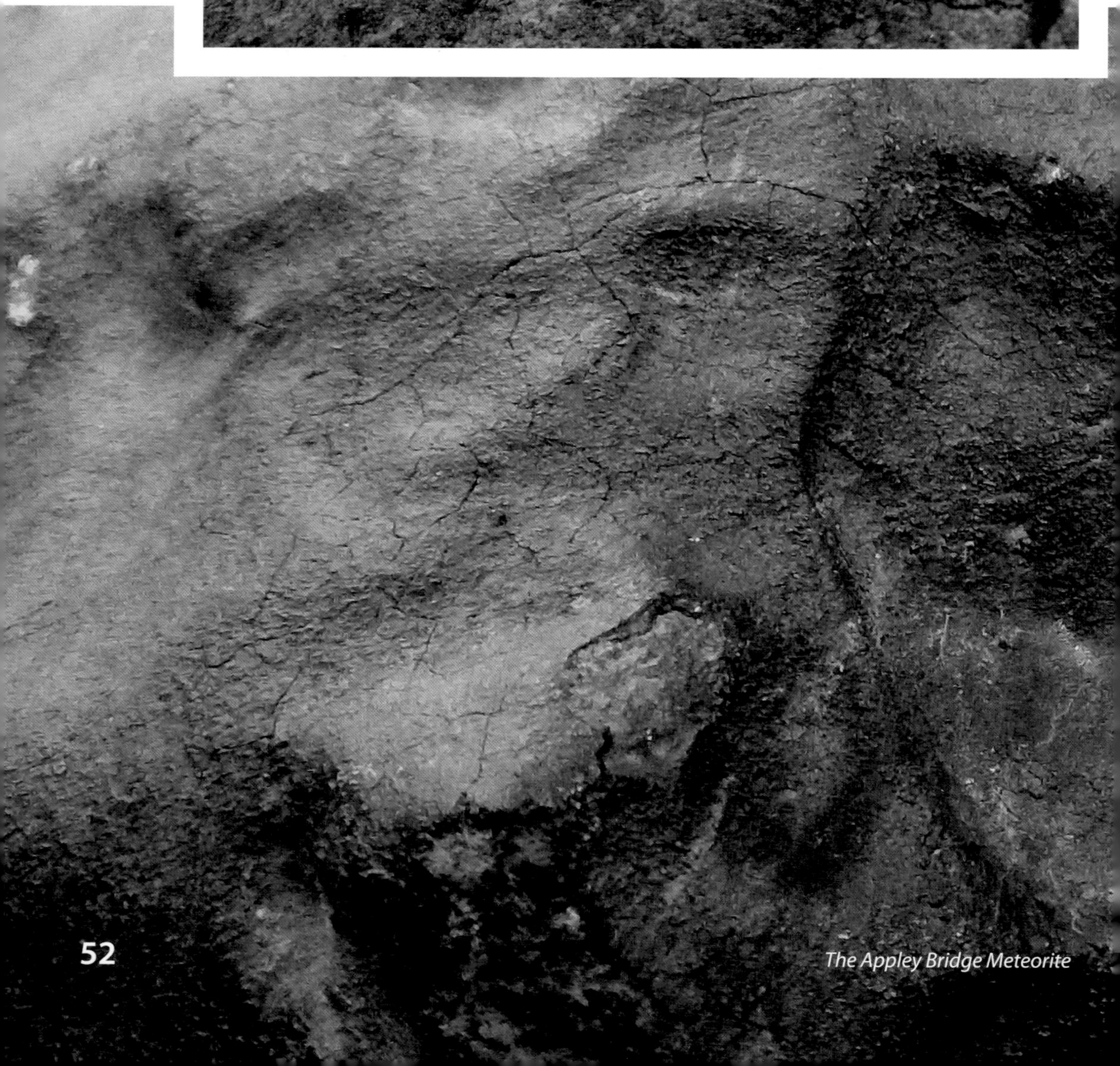

I took as many photographs as I could at various angles of both the main mass of the meteorite and the smaller piece. I then went through the various documents which were available on file, including the Register of Meteorites in the museum which was described in Chapter 4.

There was also a drawer within a locked cupboard which housed many sample containers of smaller fragments of the Appley Bridge meteorite all labelled up and referenced.

Then my encounter was over, the meteorite was carefully wrapped and boxed up. The table on which we observed and photographed the meteorite was brushed and the small fragments which came off the meteorite as it was being handled were put into a sample container, labelled up and stored in the drawer with the other smaller fragments.

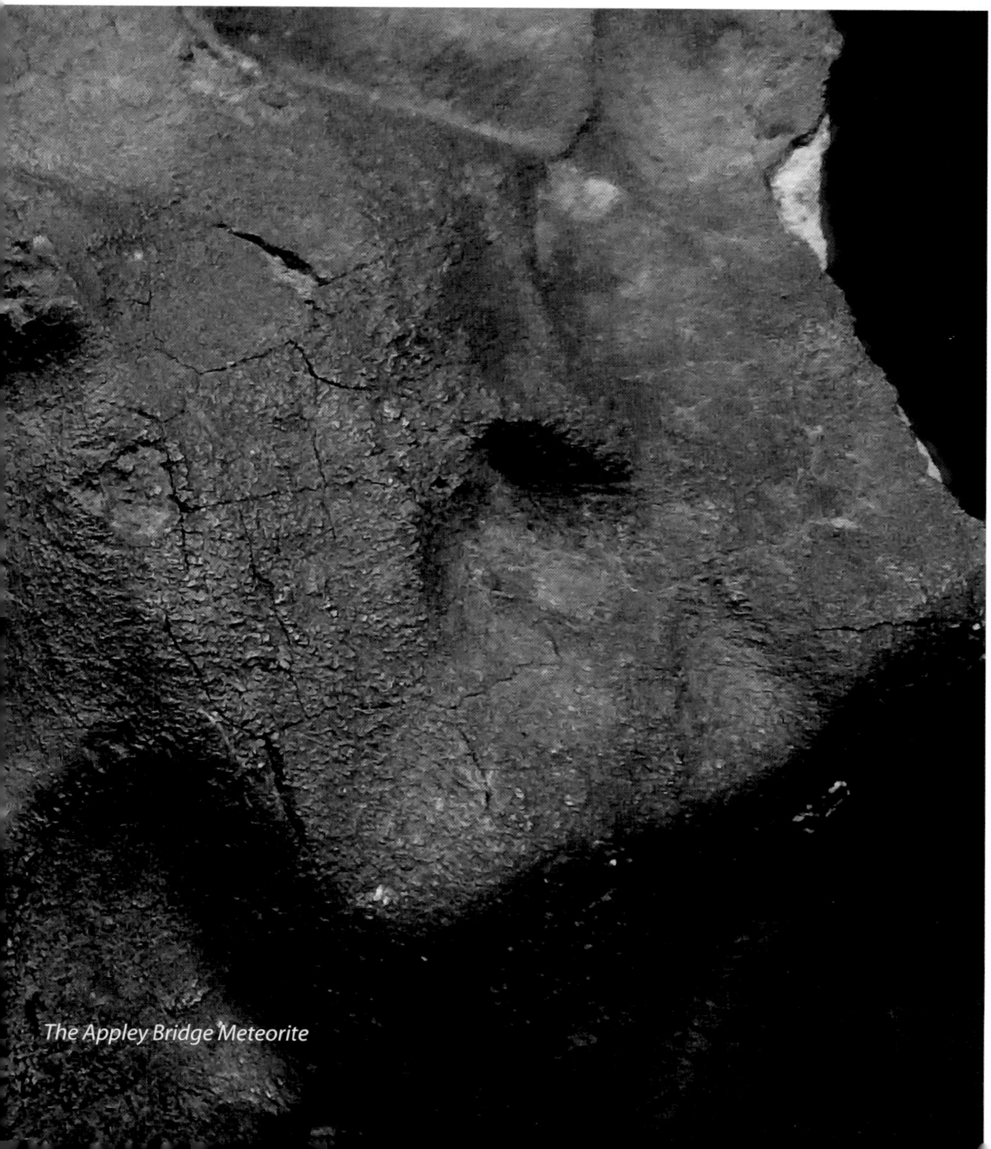

LEFT
Close up of meteorite surface showing regmaglypts.

Photographed by Russell Parry Photograph of Appley Bridge meteorite BM.1920,40 by permission of the Trustees of the Natural History Museum.

TOP RIGHT
Surface crust of the meteorite.

Photographed by Russell Parry Photograph of Appley Bridge meteorite BM.1920,40 by permission of the Trustees of the Natural History Museum

CENTRE RIGHT
Close up of surface crust.

Photographed by Russell Parry Photograph of Appley Bridge meteorite BM.1920,40 by permission of the Trustees of the Natural History Museum

BOTTOM RIGHT
Appley Bridge meteorite sample label B.M.1920. 40

Photographed by Russell Parry Photograph of Appley Bridge meteorite BM.1920,40 by permission of the Trustees of the Natural History Museum

MAIN PICTURE
The main mass of the Appley Bridge meteorite showing scale in centimetres.

Photographed by Russell Parry
Photograph of Appley Bridge meteorite BM.1920,40 by permission of the Trustees of the Natural History Museum.

RIGHT
Main mass showing numerous regmaglypts or 'thumb prints'.

Photographed by Russell Parry Photograph of Appley Bridge meteorite BM.1920,40 by permission of the Trustees of the Natural History Museum

LEFT
Main mass showing regmaglypts and surface crust.

Photographed by Russell Parry
Photograph of Appley Bridge meteorite BM.1920,40 by permission of the Trustees of the Natural History Museum

BELOW
Main mass showing regmaglypts.

Photographed by Russell Parry
Photograph of Appley Bridge meteorite BM.1920,40 by permission of the Trustees of the Natural History Museum

RIGHT
Surface of detached piece.

Photographed by Russell Parry Photograph of Appley Bridge meteorite BM.1920,40 by permission of the Trustees of the Natural History Museum.

TOP LEFT
Sample drawer with smaller samples of the Appley Bridge meteorite.

Photographed by Russell Parry Photograph of Appley Bridge meteorite BM.1920,40 by permission of the Trustees of the Natural History Museum.

MAIN PICTURE
Detached piece together with main mass.

Photographed by Russell Parry Photograph of Appley Bridge meteorite BM.1920,40 by permission of the Trustees of the Natural History Museum

THE SAGA CONTINUES

My next encounter with the Appley Bridge meteorite was a few days later on 6th November 2013, this time it was at the Manchester Museum located at the University of Manchester.

Even though this was a smaller sample than the specimens at the Natural History Museum, weighing in at just over 148 grams it was still an exciting moment to see another

RIGHT
The author with the plaster cast model of the Appley Bridge meteorite.

Photographed by Kate Sherburn
Image courtesy of The Manchester Museum

sample of the meteorite. This time no protective gloves were required to handle the specimen so it was fascinating to physically handle the meteorite with such a history and age.

Again many photographs were taken and documents observed which have been used throughout this book.

LEFT
Photo of plaster cast held at the Manchester Museum.

Photographed by Russell Parry
Image courtesy of The Manchester Museum

RIGHT
The Manchester Museum's sample of the Appley Bridge meteorite N14849.

Photographed by Russell Parry Image courtesy of The Manchester Museum

RIGHT
Close up of surface crust.

Photographed by Russell Parry Image courtesy of The Manchester Museum

CENTRE
Sample N14849 Appley Bridge meteorite.

Photographed by Kate Sherburn Image courtesy of The Manchester Museum

LEFT
Meteorite surface showing mineral content.

Photographed by Russell Parry
Image courtesy of The Manchester Museum

LEFT
Close up of surface showing mineral content.

Photographed by Russell Parry
Image courtesy of The Manchester Museum

5

BACK TO WHERE IT ALL BEGAN

I had one last place to visit on my journey through the history of the Appley Bridge meteorite and that was to find the area in which it fell.

On a beautiful sunny June evening in 2014, I travelled the few miles from my home to Halliwell Farm, a wonderful farmhouse dating from the 1600s. The current owners welcomed me into their house and I took them through all the research I had carried out to date. I mentioned the report that the meteorite landed 3 minutes walk from the farm buildings. The owner informed me of where the site of the landing had been reported to be. So, with timer set, we walked to the area and at a leisurely stroll we arrived at the spot with just under 3 minutes on the stop watch. Of course, nobody can be sure of the exact landing spot, but this just felt the right spot to me.

So my long awaited encounter with the Appley Bridge meteorite was over and my investigation into the fascinating story of the meteorite, which all started when I first moved to the little Lancashire village of Appley Bridge all those years ago was complete.

On concluding this book and reflecting on the story of the Appley Bridge meteorite, I suddenly thought something should be done to mark the up and coming 100th anniversary of the event. What better opportunity would there be to bring back the meteorite, or part of it at least, as close as possible to the landing site.

Whilst at the Wigan Local Studies, I mentioned the idea to the staff there and that started the process of arranging the plaster cast and a sample of the actual meteorite to be displayed in Wigan exactly 100 years to the day of the fall.

At the time of writing, all this is set to happen on the evening of 13th October 2014, exactly 100 years to the day. The transfer of the meteorite and plaster cast has been arranged between the Wigan Local Studies and Manchester Museum and I must thank David Gelsthorpe of the Manchester Museum and Lynda Jackson of the Museum of Wigan Life for making this happen. Exactly how many people will turn up for my talk and the display of the meteorite on the night I don't know, but for me it is another addition to the story of the Appley Bridge meteorite.

RIGHT Site of the meteorite landing under the shade of the trees? The village of Appley Bridge in the background.

© Russell Parry

APPENDIX

Further Reading

The following list of articles and publications relating to the Appley Bridge meteorite was kindly provided by permission of the Trustees of the Natural History Museum.

B. Mason, GCA, 1963, 27, p. 1011.; [Other]	Description
Denning, W F.; 1914; Nature; [Journal]; [Article]	Description
Jenkins, W C.; 1914; Nature; [Journal]; [Article]	Analysis
Mason, B & Wiik, H B.; 1964; GCA; [Journal]; [Article]	Metal composition
Sears, D W. & Axon, H J.; 1976; Meteoritics; [Journal]; [Article]	U-Pb measurements
Gale, N H.; 1979; Naturwiss.; [Journal]; [Article]	Mineralogy
Mason, B; 1963; GCA; [Journal]; [Article]	C content and d13C ratio obtained by stepped combu
Grady, M. M.; 1989; Meteoritics; [Journal]; [Article]	Pyroxene thermobarometry
H Y. & Patchen, A D.; 1989; Meteoritics; [Journal]; [Article]	Metallic copper
Rubin, A E.; 1994; Meteoritics; [Journal]; [Article]	Cosmic ray exposure age
Graf, T & Marti, K; 1994; Meteoritics; [Journal]; [Article]	Impact age (review)
Bogard, D D.; 1995; Meteoritics; [Journal]; [Article]	Thermal history
Folco, L; 1997; MAPS; [Journal]; [Article]	Bulk composition

Kallemeyn, G W.; 1989; GCA; [Journal]; [Article]	Chromite and olivine in chondrules
Johnson, C A. & Prinz, M; 1991; GCA; [Journal]; [Article]	Oxygen isotopic composition
Clayton, R N.; 1991; GCA; [Journal]; [Article]	Magnetic properties
Mordern, S J. & Collinson, D W.; 1992; EPSL; [Journal]; [Article]	Noble gas data compilation
Schultz, L & Kruse, H; 1989; Meteoritics; [Journal]; [Article]	Magnetic properties
Nagata, T; 1986; Proc. 10th Symp. on Yamato Meteorites, Mem. Nat. I; [Journal]; [Article]	Magnetic properties
Nagata, T & Funaki, M; 1987; Proc. 11th Symp. on Yamato Meteorites, Mem. Nat. I; [Journal]; [Article]	Tetrataenite
Nagata, T; 1991; Proc. NIPR Symp. Antarct. Met.; [Journal]; [Article]	Fusion crust
Genge, M J. & Grady, M. M.; 1999; MAPS; [Journal]; [Article]	Olivine and kamacite composition
Rubin, A E.; 1990; GCA; [Journal]; [Article]	

About the author

Russell Parry moved from Shrewsbury, Shropshire to Appley Bridge, Lancashire in 1991.

With a keen interest in history and astronomy the story of the Appley Bridge meteorite captured his imagination and he decided it was about time to publish the information researched over the years in time for the 100th anniversary of the meteorite fall.

Russell still lives in the area with his family and is the founder of the multi-award winning company Advanced Food Safety Limited.